20th Fighter Group

By Ron MacKay

Color By Don Greer

squadron/signal publications

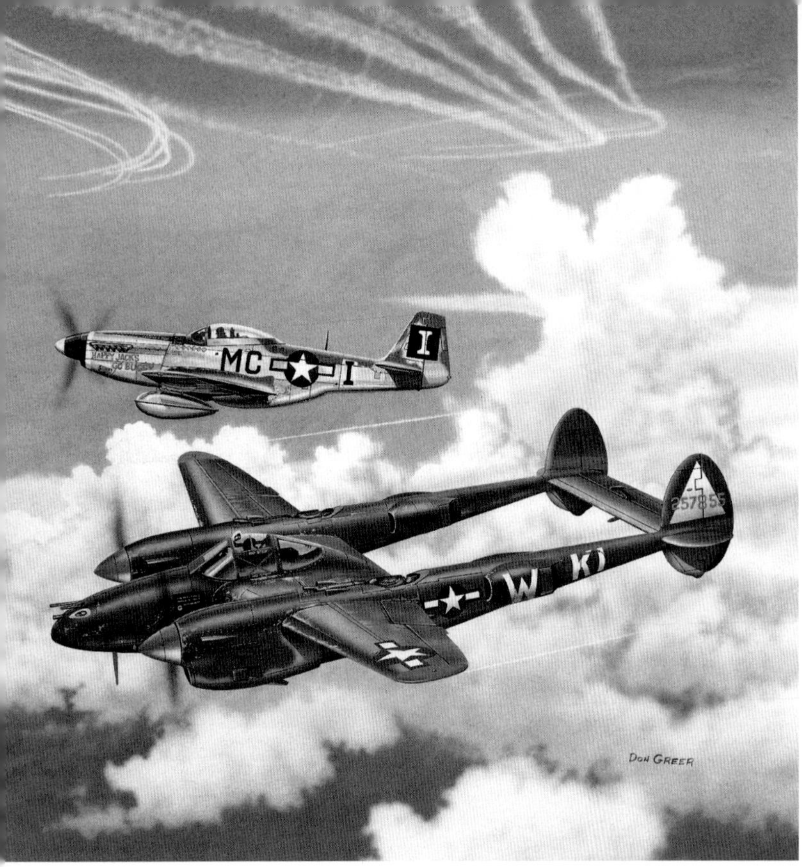

Two famous fighters of the 20th Fighter Group. The P-38J Lightning was flown by Lieutenant Royal D. Frey of the the 55th Fighter Squadron, while the P-51D, *HAPPY JACKS GO BUGGY*, was flown by Major Jack Ilfrey when he commanded the 79th Fighter Squadron.

CREDITS

Jack Ilfrey
John Measures
Bill Sharpe
Larry Davis
Dave Knight
Ray Corby
John Wilson
James Roeder

Dedication

This book is gratefully dedicated to all members of the 20th Fighter Group, and in particular to Jack Ilfrey who provided me with so much assistance in the book's completion. My thanks also to those members of the 20th FG Historical Association based in England, all long-term members of the "Friends of the Eighth," who gave their unstinted support.

ISBN 0-89747-368-X

If you have any photographs of aircraft, armor, soldiers or ships of any nation, particularly wartime snapshots, why not share them with us and help make Squadron/Signal's books all the more interesting and complete in the future. Any photograph sent to us will be copied and the original returned. The donor will be fully credited for any photos used. Please send them to:

Squadron/Signal Publications, Inc.
1115 Crowley Drive.
Carrollton, TX 75011-501010

Если у вас есть фотографии самолётов, вооружения
кораблей любой страны, особенно, снимки времён I
поделитесь с нами и помогите сделать новые книг
Эскадрон/Сигнал ещё интереснее. Мы переснимем
фотографии и вернём оригиналы. Имена приславш
будут сопровождать все опубликованные фотограф
Пожалуйста, присылайте фотографии по адресу:

Squadron/Signal Publications, Inc.
1115 Crowley Drive.
Carrollton, TX 75011-501010

軍用機、装甲車両、兵士、軍艦などの写真を 所持しておられる方はいらっしゃいませんか？どの国
ものでも結構です。作戦中に撮影されたものが特に良いのです。Squadron/Signal社の出版する刊行
において、このような写真は内容を一層充実し、興味深くすること ができます。当方にお 送り頂い
写真は、複写の後お返しいたします。出版物 中に写真を使用した場合は、必ず提供者のお 名前を明
させて頂きます。お写真は下記にご送付ください。

Squadron/Signal Publications, Inc.
1115 Crowley Drive.
Carrollton, TX 75011-501010

Introduction

The USAAF entered the Second World War with its sights set on using its heavy bombers to strike military targets in daylight. The parallel development of fighters to provide cover to and from any target, no matter how deep into the enemy hinterland, was constantly lagging far behind. The heavy armament borne by the B-17 and B-24 probably influenced the commanders to rely on this as the primary defense of the bombers, in the hopes that it would keep bomber losses at an acceptable minimum.

The P-47 Thunderbolt was in operational service by 1943, but they could not escort the bomber formations deep into central Europe, even with the belated provision for drop tanks.

The first P-38 group to arrive in England was the 20th Fighter Group, its arrival gave General Eaker (commander, 8th Bomber Command) a degree of hope that at last his bombers might have a escort worthy of the name. If not, then the entire bomber offensive was in grave danger.

The 20th Fighter Group's lineage went back to November of 1930, but the history of one of its three squadrons, the 79th Fighter Squadron, extended back to 1918. Originally created on 22 February 1918, as the 79th Aero Service Squadron at Waco, Texas, it was soon demobilized at Taliaferro Field, Texas in November. Reactivated (in an inactive status) as the 79th Observation Squadron on 1 October 1927, the unit was renamed the 79th Pursuit Squadron on 8 May 1929. The unit was called to active status on 1 April 1933.

In contrast, the 55th Fighter Squadron was created as the 55th Pursuit Squadron (inactive) on 15 November 1930. The third squadron, the 77th Fighter Squadron, was created as the 77th Observation Squadron during 1927. It redesignated as the 77th Pursuit Squadron in 1929. The 20th Pursuit Group was activated on 15 November 1930 at Mather Field, flying P-12s. Between 1932 and 1939, the Group was based at Barksdale, LA, with the P-12s being replaced by P-26s and later P-36s. A move to California, where it moved from base to base ended on 14 February 1942, when the Group moved back to Wilmington, Delaware, flying P-40s.

Although reportedly scheduled for duty with the 8th Air Force, the 20th had a long road to travel before reporting for action. During 1942, its personnel moved no less than four times before the unit learned that they were to transition into the P-38. On 1 January 1943, the unit began to transition.

The Group arrived in England aboard the QUEEN ELIZABETH in mid-August of 1943. This was a critical stage for the bombing offensive and the need for fighter cover had been dramatically proven time and time again. The presence of the 20th (and the other P-38 group the 55th Fighter Group), however, only partially met the need for a long range escort fighter capable of meeting the Luftwaffe on equal terms.

Captain Wemyss (77th Fighter Squadron Operations Officer) demonstrates a point using "pilot talk" to (L-R) Lieutenant R. Bond, Captain T. M. Williams, and Captain Kermes. Bond was Killed In Action (KIA) on 29 January 1944 and Williams was captured on 14 June 1944. Wemyss was promoted to Major in April of 1944, after assuming the Group Operations Officer position on 7 February 1944.

The Tech Sergeant talking to the other two ground crewmen appears to be dangerously close to the revolving propeller of PAPA GREMLIN. The large number on the nose indicates that this was during the unit's stateside training period.

The 20th Fighter Group arrived at its home station of Kingscliffe, Northamptonshire on 27 August 1943. To be more accurate, two squadrons moved into the base. The third, the 55th Fighter Squadron (arguably the luckiest in the circumstances) was assigned to nearby RAF Wittering, a pre-War, Permanent Station with heated brick buildings. This station was a paradise compared to Kingscliffe's wooden and tin structures, with some facilities being housed in tents. It was May of 1944, before the 55th Fighter Squadron reluctantly transferred from Wittering, having doubtless enjoyed a much more comfortable Winter in the process.

No P-38s were on immediately on hand for pilots and ground crewmen to fly and maintain. A 55th Fighter Squadron pilot, Royal D. Frey, recalls his first flights were in an RAF Beaufighter and a C-47 before two P-38s were assigned his Squadron on 8 September. By the end of the month, he had logged four and a half hours flying, just enough to regain the feel of the fighter. On one flight he was orbiting Wittering when he saw what he took to be the Fw 190 of the RAFWAFFE (captured Luftwaffe aircraft used for training) located at Collyweston (part of Wittering base). Diving down, he was surprised at being out-turned

P-38H Lightnings of the 55th Fighter Squadron, 20th Fighter Group are prepared for another mission The design on the nose of the aircraft in the foreground was the Lockheed logo. These early Lightnings were Olive Drab over Neutral Gray with a wavy camouflage demarcation.

Sergeant Brenton, Lieutenant Frey's crew chief runs up a replacement engine after Frey's aircraft had been damaged by a Bf 110 on 29 January 1944. The P-38, named *Stardust,* was lost over Germany when Frey had to bail out after losing both engines.

by the "Fw." The incident was even more embarrassing when, after landing, he discovered that his adversary was merely a Miles Martinet trainer whose general outline matched that of Kurt Tank's thoroughbred. He further embarrassed his Squadron Commander, Major McGovern, by landing over the parade-ground where General Kepner (Commander, 8th Fighter Command) was carrying out a review. Frey's snappy peel off disrupted the proceedings and annoyed the General. A reprimand, grounding for one week and confinement to base was a chastening act for Frey, who thought he would make a 'hot-shot' P-38 pilot once committed to combat.

The nineteen year-old pilot's experience was perhaps typical of the

Pilots of the 20th Fighter Group run past a P-38H on the way to their aircraft at Kingscliffe during September of 1943. (via Larry Davis)

Lieutenant Jim "Slick" Morris poses in front of his P-38 named *Til We Meet Again.* He became one of the first 20th Fighter Group Aces scoring four kills on one mission (8 February 1944). He was assigned to the 77th Fighter Squadron and had a total of eight kills before he was shot down on 7 July 1944 and captured.

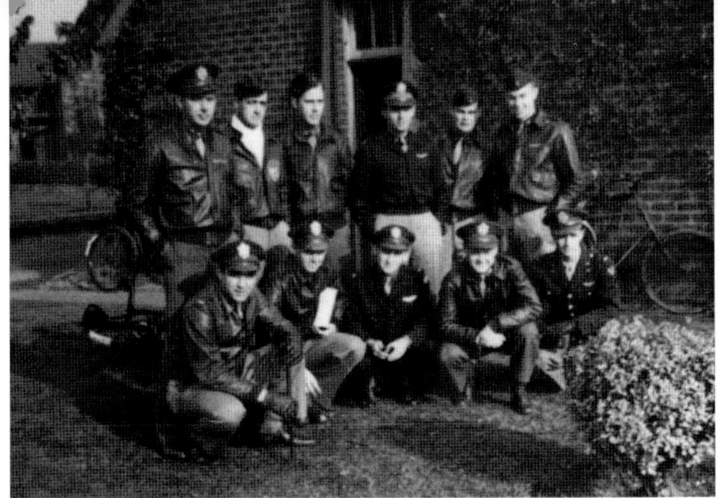

Of this group of 55th Fighter Squadron original pilots, four would be Killed in Action by February of 1944, a fifth would be killed during November and two would be captured by April of 1944.

pace of training since his squadron had only six P-38s by late November. Despite this, some of the Group had flown combat missions, not from Kingscliffe, but from Nuthampstead some sixty miles south. This base was occupied by the 55th Fighter Group who, although arriving in England after the 20th Fighter Group, had been committed to action in October. On 3 November, nine 79th Fighter Squadron pilots were deployed there to take part in five missions between 5 and 11 November. They were replaced by 77th Fighter Squadron personnel who flew five missions (up to 1 December) before selected 55th Fighter Squadron pilots took over to fly two missions.

The overall experiences for those involved were somewhat depressing, none more so than on the first mission. Four P-38s aborted on the way out, and another four inadvertently followed Major Wilkins when he turned back. The tenth pilot, Lieutenant Fall tried to slot into the 38th Fighter Squadron formation with no success, so he also came home. A double mission on 7 November witnessed few aborts, but two pilots were listed as Missing In Action (MIA), Major Wilkins disappeared without trace after taking-off late and Captain Cummings bailed out over the North Sea while being escorted home with one engine out, the result of battle damage. A long "Winter of Discontent" had begun for the Group. The sole enemy contact so far were two Fw 190s, bounced without effect.

The next interceptions were not until 25 November, when Fw 190s came down near Lille and were engaged by a flight from the 79th Fighter Squadron. Lieutenant Lane emerged from the fight on one engine, but fatally crashed near Nuthampstead when his other engine caught fire and the P-38 went in. The next day, Major Johnson extracted some revenge when he knocked down a Do-217, but three days later Lieutenant Hascall disappeared over Aschaffenburg. A fourth loss occurred on 30 November, when Lieutenant Bob Thomas ditched; although he survived the water landing, he subsequently died in a German hospital. Finally, Lieutenant Jack Gard was downed by an Bf 109 on 1 December.

A P-38H-5 of the 55th Fighter Squadron prepares to taxi out for another mission during early 1943. (via Larry Davis)

It seems incredible that Lieutenant Fogg (79th Fighter Squadron) survived this crash-landing, let alone the fire that consumed the fuselage pod. The crash took place on 4 March 1944 at Spanhoe. Fogg was shot down and became a POW on 30 April 1944.

Early Operations

The first full mission in the Group's own right was launched on 28 December. It was a Low Countries Fighter Sweep. The thirty-four assigned and five spare pilots were led by Colonel Jack Jenkins (55th Fighter Group Deputy Commander), the sole opposition coming from flak. The next day, Jenkins had to abort and the first direct Group command was assumed by Major Montgomery (Group Air Executive) for what was another quiet run over Belgium, although thirteen aircraft landed away from base.

"The Big League of Sky Fighting" was entered on the last day of 1943. It began tragically for the 55th Fighter Squadron. Their pilots were ordered to fly over to Kingscliffe for joint briefing and assembly with the other squadrons. Lieutenant John Crago struck an obstruction on take-off and crashed after reaching Kingscliffe. Strangely, official records show his loss on a "training flight" despite his departure on the first stage of a mission. The line on the map stretched far down to the Southwest French coast, the Group giving target cover to bombers

Mechanics and armorers work on a P-38H of the 20th Fighter Group in the open at Kingscliffe. The wooden work stands were common at this time. (via Larry Davis)

attacking Bordeaux and La Rochelle; also involved were the 55th Fighter Group and the pioneer P-51 Group the 354th Fighter Group. The sole recorded interception was Lieutenant Graham's attack on two Fw 190s in which he landed strikes on one before it swept into the clouds. Fully sixteen aircraft landed in Southern England with Lieutenant Garrett's fuel drying up and forcing him to belly-in.

The Group was now blooded in its own right and with the continued emphasis upon attacking German industry over Western Europe, the Kingscliffe fliers would be put to a stern, prolonged, and rather unrewarding, test during the first three months of 1944.

Of the nine January missions, six involved target support and three provided cover as the bombers withdrew from the target. Kiel (4 January) saw only thirty-two of the forty-two P-38s reaching that far. A forty minute patrol at 30,000 feet was negative, although a Do-217 and Ju 88 were driven off. High winds drifted some of the pilots south of track and they emerged from the clouds as far apart as Calais and Cherbourg. All but one regained English soil, the unlucky one being Lieutenant Hamilton, who probably ran out of fuel after trailing Lieutenant Baker to Cherbourg. In addition Lieutenant Higginbotham was Missing In Action (MIA) in the target area and was later confirmed as Killed in Action (KIA).

Sky Cowboy was flown by Lieutenant Walker Whiteside (77th Fighter Squadron) who was assigned on 17 November 1943. He racked up a total of 236 combat hours and became a flight leader in June of 1944. He was Killed In Action (KIA) on 6 August 1944.

Major Bob Riemensnider poses in front of his P-38 named "Bobby". His aircraft mission tally reveals thirty-five escort missions, twelve top cover missions, eight fighter sweeps and nine bombing missions.

Kiel was revisited next day and although damage claims were submitted by Major Montgomery and Lieutenant Taylor (the latter also downing an Fw 190 harassing Lieutenant Frey) the battle ended in the Luftwaffe's favor. Lieutenants Altman and French (55th Fighter Squadron) and Lieutenant Carbajo (77th Fighter Squadron) were all declared MIA with opnly French surviving as a POW. Lieutenant Frey lost his hydraulic system and was fortunate to survive close-combat maneuvers with two fighters; the second was on his tail when knocked down by Lieutenant Taylor from head-on.

Over the next nine days, three missions were launched, two being completed. Over Worms (7 January) Lieutenant Bill Taylor downed one of three rocket-bearing Bf 110s. In between then and 14 January, a momentous mission was dispatched to the Focke Wulf plant at Oschersleben. As with much of the assigned fighter cover, the 20th Fighter Group's intended support of that part of the bomber force attacking the MIAG plant at Brunswick was thwarted by clouds which rose so high that the fighters were still in the clouds at 34,000 feet, whereupon Major Montgomery turned for home.

Having suffered a terrible beating on 11 January, with sixty bombers and five fighters missing, the 8th Air Force drew in its claws on the 14th

This P-38J of the 77th Fighter Squadron suffered battle damage to the vertical stabilizer. The aircraft carried several names with *Libluf Nanny* on the nose and *Roxie* on the engine cowling. (via Larry Davis)

Roy Scrutchfield took his crew chief up in the cleared out space behind the cockpit on a test flight. He demonstrated the technique of switching off the engines and restarting them in flight, however, the engines refused to restart. Luckily, neither man was injured in the resulting forced landing, although the Lightning was a write-off.

and hit the Pas de Calais just across the Channel. The 20th Fighter Group headed for the Rouen/Le havre region, splitting into squadron to cover different sections. The bombing altitude was only 12,000 feet

Lieutenant Colonel Russell Gustke joined the 20th Fighter Group in February of 1944. After serving as 77th Fighter Squadron Operations Officer and later Squadron Commander, he became Deputy Group Commander on 18 December 1944. He stepped down after completing his third combat tour on 19 April 1945.

Jack Ilfrey flew this P-38 named *HAPPY JACK'S GO BUGGY*. At this point aircraft carried eight kill markings as well as two locomotive kills that he had personally strafed and destroyed.

This P-38J (MC-K, serial 267200) of the 79th Fighter Squadron, flown by Flight Officer Byrd, ran off the runway when the port main landing gear failed on landing. The aircraft has also suffered some battle damage to the leading edge of the horizontal stabilizer. The port engine was still running at the time of the crash while the feathered propeller on the starboard engine indicates that it was shut down prior to landing. The Lightning was scrapped on 10 January 1944.

A group of 55th Fighter Squadron pilots with Doc Wedemeyer (seated, left) during early 1944. Included are (L-R) Art Rowley, Gene Geiger (POW), Jack Yelton (POW), Jack Frazier (KIA 24 January 1944), and Jack Taylor (killed 10 February 1944).

MajorJohn C. Watkins was the 20th Fighter Group's first Air Executive Officer. His operational career was cut short when he was declared Missing In Action of 7 November 1943. He took off late and was never seen again.

Lieutenant Harry Bisher (55th Fighter Squadron) demonstrates the typical high altitude flight attire issued to P-38 pilots. Bisher was declared Missing In Action (MIA) on 4 March 1944, but was able to evade and returned to England by June.

This bicycle and cart was designed by Staff Sergeants Ed Beck and Harry Linden of the 55th Fighter Squadron to transport the heavier items of their specialist equipment.

(Above & Left) Captain Maurice McLary of the 55th Fighter Squadron bellied in at Rougham on 29 January 1944. He points out the bullet holes in his Lightning to the commander of the 94th Bomb Group, the unit that occupied the base at Rougham. McLary later became commander of the 77th Fighter Squadron.

with cover at this level. Enemy attempts to penetrate the fighter screen resulted in Colonel Russell and F/O Byrd each downing an Fw 190. Lieutenant Nichols (79th Fighter Squadron), flying in the same flight, warned Russell to break, picking up the Fw 190 homing in on him and shooting it down. Elsewhere, Lieutenant Mednick (79th Fighter Squadron) heavily damaged a Bf 109, as did Lieutenant Hanzo (also of the 79th Fighter Squadron). At Rouen, Captain Meyer (79th Fighter Squadron) damaged two Bf 109s flying together, while his fellow-squadron pilot, Lieutenant Lefevre, damaged a third. Captain Graham saved Lieutenant Gall by driving off two Bf 109s that were closing on him. The flight had just been bounced and Lieutenant Wyman was already heading for home with one engine out, He finally had to crash land at base, his P-38 being wrecked. A similar bounce on the 79th Fighter Squadron's Blue Flight cost Lieutenant Archer, who sadly joined the steadily growing list of pilots Killed In Action (KIA).

In the first ten weeks of combat the ratio of Kills to Losses was in the enemy's favor, by a ratio of four to thirteen, with two of the latter over England. On 29 January, that unfavorable position would be altered, but still at a human cost to the Group. The P-38s were displaying basic and potentially lethal failures with the main problem involving the Allison engines. As an example, hastily applied power often resulted in con-rods malfunctioning; losing fifty percent power was bad enough, but when it occurred in the middle of a combat, the pilot's survival chances were drastically reduced. Then, the P-38's roll-rate and diving performance was poor compared to the Fw 190s and Bf 109s. Pilot comfort was equally poor with the cockpit heating system not being worthy of the name (airborne ice-wagons was the aptly applied nickname to the

***STUBBORN VIRGIN* of the 55th Fighter Squadron carried an impressive scoreboard of fighter sweeps,, escort, top cover and bombing missions. This P-38 was flown by Captain Serros, who was killed in Action on 2 November 1944.**

Captain Merin "Doc" Wedemeyer (55th Fighter Squadron) cycles past camouflaged buildings during the squadron's stay at RAF Wittering.

This 20th Fighter Group P-38J Droop-snoot displays ten mission symbols on the fuselage behind the bombardier's window. The name, *EZE DOES IT,* refers to Lieutenant Herschel Ezell, who served as lead bombardier with the 20th after serving a tour with a B-17 group.

Lockheed design by no less a figure than Colonel Cy Wilson, who served both as Deputy and full Group Commander). With pilots having to react in split seconds to any combat scenario, the sapping of their energy by the temperatures experienced at 25,000 feet and 30,000 feet (the average patrol height) inevitably dulled the mind and the mental capacity to act promptly.

Another short-haul to Cherbourg was assigned for 21 January and completed without incident, unlike the mission three days later. With Frankfurt cloud-covered, the bombers hit a target of opportunity. While covering their approach to the enemy coast, the 55th Fighter Squadron was bounced between Ghent and Lille. Captain McAuley turned on one of the Fw 190s and knocked pieces off, following up by taking on a sec-

This 79th Fighter Squadron P-38J Droop Snoot carries full D-Day markings along with Yellow bands on the fuselage, Yellow cowling fronts and wing roots. The aircraft is carrying a fin stabilized drop tank on the starboard pylon. This was probably a fuel tank that was used as a "bomb", a forerunner of the later napalm bomb.

This P-38J of the 77th FIghter Squadron, flown by Lieutenant Clark, has a section missing from its port rudder. The aircraft made it to an emergency field where it shared the grass with a P-51 and a P-47.

(Above & Below) *California Cutie* carries full D-Day invasion stripes. She was flown by Lieutenant Loehnert (on nose wheel) and crewed by Tech Sergeant Dickerson. The aircraft carried the squadron code KI-S.

Captain Jack Ilfrey and one of his ground crew inspect the damage to the wingtip of his Lightning, after he collided with a Bf 109 on 24 May 1944. Only the P-38 survived the mid-air collision.

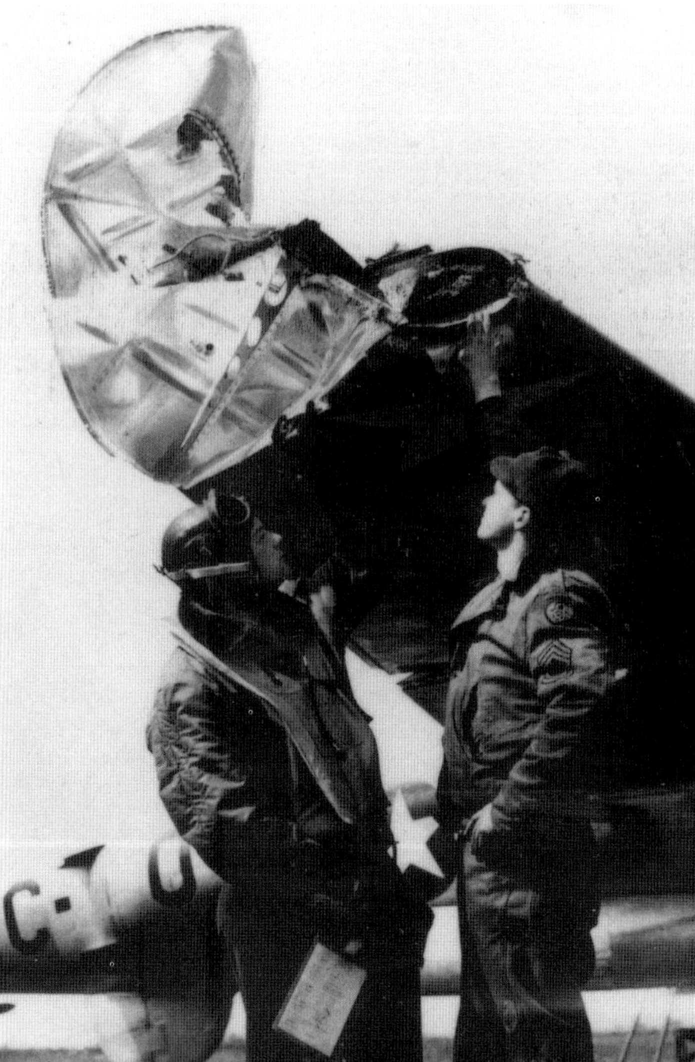

Major Carl Jackson's P-38 carried the name *"Jack"* and five playing cards, all Jacks. The Lightning carried mission markings for twelve top cover and one kill. Jackson took over for Major Ott (who was killed on 30 January 1944) to become a POW only three weeks later.

Major Franklin stands by the nose of his P-38 named Strictly Stella's Baby, named in honor of his wife. He completed his tour of 200 combat hours in May of 1944. He commanded the 79th Fighter Squadron.

A line of P-38s taxi on the grass at Kingscliffe. The first four aircraft carry 77th Fighter Squadron codes, while the last two do not have their codes painted on as yet. The vertical fins are all heavily exhaust stained.

Captain Lindol Graham (left) with four other pilots poses in front of his P-38J *Susie*. The panels on the legs of the flying suits held mission information placards. Graham was killed on 18 March 1944. Before his death, he added at least two more kills to the three carried on the nose of his Lightning.

ond, which he destroyed. Captain McLary also downed one and damaged the second of a Rotte (pair). Lieutenant Baker engaged a Fw 190 as it pursued Lieutenant Ahern, igniting its drop-tank, which blew off.

Unhappily each Squadron came home short one pilot. Lieutenant Cal Hart (55th Fighter Squadron) went down after flak crippled one engine, which then caught fire. During the air battle Lieutenant Frazier disap-

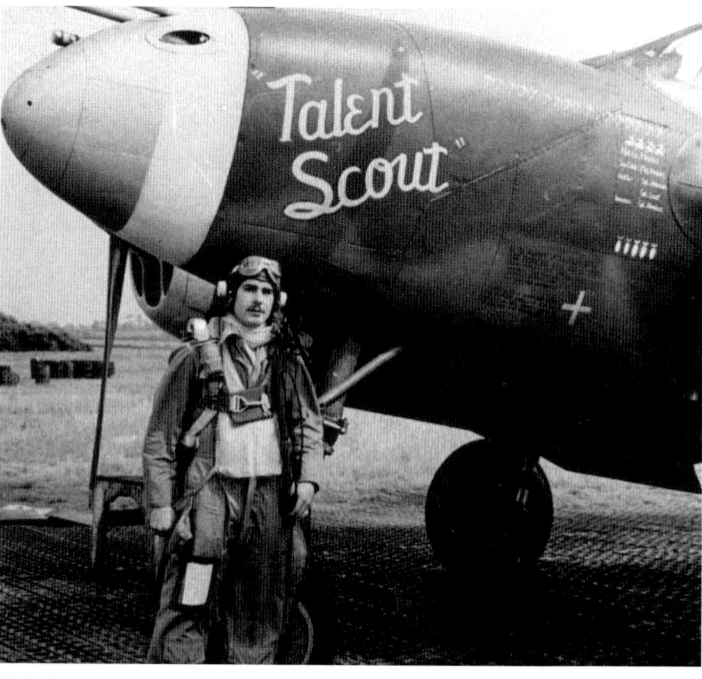

This P-38, named *"Talent Scout"*, was flown by Lieutenant Denbo. He was later killed on 12 August 1944 while flying P-51s.

peared into cloud, an Fw 190 on his tail; he did not survive. Lieutenant Hatrig was desperately trying to avoid combat, on one engine and hug-

This P-38J was the third aircraft named *Murph* by Major McLary. The absence of nose and cowling colors suggest that this was during early 1944. The aircraft was coded KI-V. The aircraft was lost on 22 June while being flown by Lieutenant Pierson, who was listed as Killed In Action.

Lieutenant Rod Watson poses with his P-38J named *Dotty* during August of 1944, shortly before the unit converted to P-51s. Some of the Mustangs for the 55th Fighter Squadron are visible in the background.

ging the bomber formation, when the Fw 190s struck. He also slipped into the clouds and the next report on him came via the Air Sea Rescue (ASR) launch crew who picked him up dead out of the North Sea.

Hart was the sole pilot to survive. He was forced to bale out and, as he did so, his dinghy-pack broke away (fortunately he descended over land). Once down, he succeeded in making contact with the Resistance and plans were put in motion to move him Southward to the Spanish border. One day he was taken to Lille to have his picture taken for an Identity Card. His guide coolly lined up in a queue of German soldiers waiting their turn in the photo booth. When her turn came she beckoned to Hart to take her place and enter the booth; she then fended off the soldiers sharp reaction with humorous remarks. That same evening in a night-club Hart accidentally knocked a German officer's revolver holster

Capt Jack Ilfrey in the cockpit of his P-38. With the rear opening top panel and push down side panels, bailing out of a P-38 was a cumbersome and time consuming procedure.

off his chair back, but with no serious consequences for the (probably unnerved) American:

Moved on to Paris and then to Montauban, the first attempt to cross the Spanish border was a failure. There would be no second attempt because while Hart was at the home of his contact's relations, a Gestapo-led squad of soldiers broke in and took him into custody. No one else was arrested, but why the Germans appeared to think the American airman was on his own was puzzling (his contact, Helen Himpe, was instrumental in moving Harry Bisher and Bob Montgomery through to England the following June).

The final two January missions (29 and 30 January) saw the Luftwaffe engaged in force. Frankfurt and Brunswick were "deep in there" and

This overall Natural Metal P-38J of the 79th Fighter Squadron suffered a failed landing gear after the 12 May 1944 mission. The pilot was Lieutenant Al Learned.

Lieutenant Hartig poses with his ground crew along side THELMA. The baby face in the star suggests the aircraft was named for his daughter. He was lost on 24 January 1944, while on his fourth mission. He bailed out over the sea, only to drown.

strong enemy reaction could be expected. The Group's response was solid. The initial direct clash on Frankfurt occurred as the Squadrons were dis-engaging from target-cover. The 79th Fighter Squadron's Captain Graham, latched onto an Fw 190 boring in on the bombers, a tail-chase ending in a fusillade of cannon shells and bullets tearing his opponent apart. Then, while guarding some crippled stragglers, Graham attacked two Fw 190s scoring strikes on one of them. He chased the pair for a few minutes prior to closing to lethal range; first the wingman and then the leader were shredded by his accurate fire.

(Below and Right) *Pistol Packin' Mama*, a P-38H-5-LO, was assigned to the 55th Fighter Squadron while at RAF Wittering. The aircraft was coded KI-K. (via Larry Davis)

MC-B crashed shortly after D-Day on 19 June 1944. The aircraft was assigned to Lieutenant Bradshaw, but was being flown by Lieutenant Peterson

Captain Gatterdam (also 79th Fighter Squadron) led his flight in pursuit of two Fw 190s and crippled one, while Major Ott (79th Fighter Squadron) successfully bounced a Bf 110. The 77th Fighter Squadron

(Right) Ed Beck (in cockpit) and Harry Linden were engineering specialists with the 55th Fighter Squadron. The "No Step" marking was on the canopy framing in White.

joined in the destruction with Lieutenants Machen and Minton taking out one Me 210 with Major Ott and Lieutenant Whiteside destroying its partner. Whiteside nailed a Bf 109 as it closed on Ott, whose P-38 was now in trouble with one engine out. The next kill had a tragic outcome for Lieutenants Bond and Flynn (77th Fighter Squadron). They jointly attacked a Me 210, which fell away in flames, but as the P-38s turned away they collided, neither pilot baling out. Lieutenant Frey's short combat career took an upward surge on this mission. He picked out an Me 110, disabled the rear gunner and sent the enemy fighter down in flames. Return fire so damaged his right engine that upon return to base it had to be replaced. Two other squadron pilots, Lieutenant Hallberg and Captain Serros, closed off the Group's account by destroying yet another Bf 110. A total of ten kills and two probables would have been a great morale booster to the Kingscliffe men, had it not been for the pilots who were listed as MIA. In addition to Bond and Flynn, Lieutenant Moss (79th Fighter Squadron) ended up a POW after vacating his crippled P-38 and F/O Harper (also 79th Fighter Squadron) was probably killed in his cockpit when shells from an Fw 190 burst all round his center fuselage.

One pilot landing away from base was Captain Maurice McLary. He had suffered damage to his right engine and hydraulic system, and bellied-in at Rougham, home for the B-17s of the 94th Bomb Group.

30 January was another day of mixed fortunes as forty-eight P-38s escorted the bombers to the Dummersee area; by then eight aircraft had

Captain Don Reihmer of the 77th Fighter Squadron poses on the nose of his P-38, *Filly From Phily IV*. He was forced down over the Baltic Sea on 4 August 1944, while flying a P-51, and was picked up by a neutral ship.

Captain Bill Smith (55th Fighter Squadron) originally joined the 20th Fighter Group in November of 1942, but was transferred following an accident. He was reassigned in June of 1943 and served as squadron operations officer for the 79th and 55th Fighter Squadrons until October of 1944. He flew a P-38 named *OKIE-BLOKE* (MC-N) with the 79th Fighter Squadron.

An overshoot on landing and soft ground led to this accident. Luckily the cockpit framing was strong enough to survive the impact and the pilot escaped without injury. The code letters identifies this Lightning as being a 55th Fighter Squadron aircraft.

Lieutenant Royal Frey of the 55th Fighter Squadron poses on the wing of a Beech Staggerwing transport. The C-Type hangar in the background identifies this as RAF Wittering. The Staggerwing is carrying the Red surround national insignia.

aborted. Numerous engine failures among the remaining fighters added to the difficulty of giving adequate cover. Four enemy aircraft were destroyed. The first an Me 210 was claimed by Captain Gatterdam and Lieutenant Martin. After this engagement, they escorted Lieutenant Gall's crippled fighter home. Major Ott downed an Fw 190 and a Do-217 while Lieutenants Fall and Ruark killed another Do-217. Return fire from Ott's second victim disabled one engine and he turned for home with Lieutenants Orr, Fall and Ruark covering. The small formation, however, was bounced by eight Fw 190s led by Lieutenant Karl - Heinz Willius (known as Charlie in his unit). With his good engine smoking, Ott fell away into the undercast, as did Lieutenant Fall; only Fall survived. (Willius was KIA over the Zuiderzee on 8 April and his Fw 190, with his body still inside was disinterred many years later). Lieutenant Martin was badly wounded in the head and neck by an Fw 190. Barely able to focus on his instruments from the loss of blood and with one engine malfunctioning, he just made it to the emergency airfield at Woodbridge, promptly collapsing after getting out of the cockpit.

This tangled wreck of a 55th Fighter Squadron Lightning after it was righted from an inverted position. The crash took place sometime between 6 June and 20 July 1944.

Landing after the final D-Day mission in poor visibility, Major George Wemyss came down short of the runway. Both propellers were torn off the Lightning, but Wemyss walked away from the crash uninjured.

A critical period of operations now loomed for the U.S. Strategic and Tactical Air Forces (USSTAF). Between late February and the end of April, continuous and increased pressure was to be exerted on the Luftwaffe, both in the air and on the ground. Defeat of this still formidable force was an absolute prerequisite for the projected Invasion of Western Europe.

The Group's first February mission saw a change from long-range bomber escort, cover being given to B-26s attacking Triqueville. These, however, were not to be seen either at the rendezvous point nor over the target. Visual sighting was limited by heavy cloud, causing the Group to return home. No action was reported on the next two missions although Lieutenant Durand (77th Fighter Squadron) failed to return from Frankfurt (4 February). Continued mechanical problems were forcing many pilots to abort, with the low point being reached on 4 February, when twenty-four out of forty-eight had to turn back. Indeed, some 138 aircraft would abort missions during February.

A foretaste of the type of action which would transform the Group's combat situation in April was experienced on 5 February. On the way in Colonel Russell noticed aircraft taking off below. He detached the 77th Fighter Squadron to attack, with the 55th Fighter Squadron acting as their cover. A Fw 200 Kondor patrol bomber and a He 111 were

The missing wingtip, scraped leading edge, dented propeller spinner and engine cowling all show just how narrow an escape Lieutenant Ed Wasil had. His P-38J struck a tree while he was strafing an airfield near Liege on 1 May 1944. Two others in the 55th Fighter Squadron were shot down by flak on this same mission.

Pilots of the 55th Fighter Squadron including Captain Serros (3rd from left). Other pilots include (L-R) Lieutenants Pearson, Conners, Hallberg, Cruikshand and Ford. Only Hallberg and Ford survived the war.

This was the result of "flat hatting" with a P-38. Lieutenant L. Taylor went too low, sturck a revetment and crashed. The wreckage was scattered over hundreds of yards and the pilot was killed.

Lieutenant Frey (Left) was shot down and became a POW on 10 February 1944. Lieutenant John Crago (Right) was killed in a take off accident on 31 December 1943. Both pilots were assigned to the 55th Fighter Squadron)

Colonel Wilson's P-38 took a shell hit on its windshield, which badly restricted the pilot's vision. Despite the damage, Wilson was able to make a safe landing. The aircraft was later ditched by Lieutenant Klink on 16 July 1944.

Lieutenant (later Captain) Roy Scrutchfield's P-38J, *Jeanne,* carried sharkmouth markings. The aircraft suffered a nose wheel failure on landing. Scrutchfield joined the 20th in September of 1943, completing one tour (221 combat hours) as 55th Fighter Squadron Operations Officer on 3 November 1944.

Lieutenant Royal D. Frey flew this P-38J (KI-V) which was named Stardust. The aircraft had a White Star on the wheel cover. (via Larry Davis)

This P-38J was flown by Colonel Cy Wilson on or near D-Day. Colonel Wilson was commander of the 55th Fighter Squadron, but assumed command of the Group on 25 June, replacing Colonel Rau, who returned home.

Captain Jack Ilfrey was shot down near Angers, France on 13 June 1944, but was able to regain Allied lines in a matter of days, after being outfitted by the French to pass as a French civilian.

A relaxed group of pilots from the 55th Fighter Squadron. The squadron commander, Major McAuley was forth from right. The pilot in the center is wearing RAF style flying boots.

downed in the speedily executed assault. A second French target next day was uneventful for all but Lieutenant Byrd (79th Fighter Squadron) whose P-38 was fatally crippled by flak and crashed after its pilot baled out.

The emphasis now shifted to missions against Germany. There was a good start to this period for Lieutenant James Morris (77th Fighter Squadron) while on a mission to Frankfurt (8 February). Flying in the Group Leader's Flight he spotted an Bf 109; Colonel Montgomery engaged but failed in his attack, due to a frosted windscreen. Then Morris took over and knocked it down. A locomotive's career was ended when Morris shot up its boiler. A short time later, two Fw 190s were seen taking off; this was as far as either got since both were also picked off by Morris. The finale of this eventful mission came near Denain when Morris, by now separated from the other flight elements, took on an Bf 109 coming in from the right, circling onto its tail and finishing it off. This total of four kills in one mission was a record at this point of 8th Fighter Command operations. Morris' Flight companion, Lieutenant Bob Frakes had previously suffered turbo failure and never made it back, as did Lieutenant Rierson (79th Fighter Squadron). Both became POWs but Frakes's experience at the hands of the Gestapo (having evaded immediate capture and being sheltered by the Resistance before he and his helper were betrayed) is worthy of a more detailed description. He, like Lieutenant Hart, was to pass through the extremes of optimism and despair in the next few months. His P-38 had crashed in an apple orchard between Charleroi and Namur and he had been pulled from the cockpit by Belgians who quickly spirited him away on a sledge and later attempted to set his broken leg. While concealed, he passed on his knowledge of flak positions, barracks and other facilities on German airfields for Resistance use in making attacks. Plans were ultimately made for Bob's return to England and he, with his guide Jeanne, moved to Brussels where they rendezvoused with another linkman known as Charlie. The ever present threat of German infiltrators within the Resistance came to the fore a few minutes after all three had

Pilots and ground crews found a pleasant use for P-38 drop tanks, converting them to boats for recreational use.

(Above and Right) This A-20 Havoc was one of a number of "operationally retired" aircraft which served as group "hacks." Carrying 55th Fighter Squadron codes, it flew for many months before finally being abandoned after suffering a landing accident in which it damaged the nose gear.

entered a small car and drove off. They were stopped and surrounded by SS troops who dragged them out. Charlie, however, was the only one who left without hand-cuffs.

Interrogated relentlessly and threatened with being treated as a spy if he did not reveal more details about Jeanne and her comrades, Bob was finally brought face to face with her horribly tortured and barely living body, but he still held out with "name, rank and serial number." It was many weeks before his final release to the Luftwaffe and eventual incarceration in Stalag Luft III, Sagan. As he left the Gestapo prison he sighted Charlie, but this time he was wearing a German uniform, (Bob's last report on Jeanne was that she was still alive in another prison).

On the morning of the 10 February, Lieutenant Frey took off for what would be his eleventh and final mission of his combat tour. Rendezvous with the bombers was made near Dummersee, but already (and apart from those aborting) the Group was short one pilot; one of a group of ten Fw 190s had slipped in behind Lieutenant Lundin (55th Fighter Squadron) and killed him. Heading for home in separate flights, Captain McLary's (which included Frey) attacked a formation of up to six twin-engined fighters surrounding one P-38. In the ensuing battle, McLary downed an Bf 110 and an Me 410. Elsewhere, another 55th Fighter Squadron Flight Leader, Lieutenant Taylor claimed an Bf 109 as did

(Right) *Big Tin Bird* was a war-weary B-17E Flying Fortress that served with the 20th Fighter Group as a group "hack" between 1944 and VE-Day. All armament was stripped from the bomber and the engine cowlings were painted Yellow.

Lieutenant Morris discusses the upcoming mission with his crew chief, T/SGT McCarland. The P-38J was named *Black Barney* and was assigned to Colonel Russell (Group Commander). The nose wheel tire has a diamond tread pattern.

A P-38J Lightning of the 77th Fighter Squadron undergoing maintenance on the ramp. One group is refueling the aircraft, while the crew chief discusses assignments with the rest of the maintenance crew. The fuselage access ladder is fully extended.

The ground crew of *Bobcat II* pose in front of the P-38J flown by Colonel Bob Meyers (79th Fighter Squadron). The aircraft was coded MC-R . It was later lost while being flown by Lieutenant H. Watson (he was captured) on 25 May 1944.

"The men behind the men who made the headlines." This is a group of ground crewmen of the 77th Fighter Squadron, just before D-Day. The P-38J in the background has severe exhaust staining on the vertical stabilizer which has nearly covered the White squadron marking. There are a number of 150 gallon underwing fuel tanks stacked at the right, These tanks were unique to the P-38, although there were instances when other fighters adopted the tanks to fit their underwing racks.

Pilots sycnronise their watches during the D-Day briefing. Colonel Wilson is third from right, while Lieutenant Riemensnider is to his right and Major McLary is to his left.

Captains Meyer and Jackson (79th Fighter Squadron).

The claims for kills was completed by Lieutenant Lefevre (79th Fighter Squadron) who ran into an Me 410 as he returned home on the deck with super-charger trouble. Seven damaged claims were also submitted. What could not be confirmed was Lieutenant Frey's second kill, for the simple reason he was already in enemy hands. He had closed on an Bf ll0 heading westward, using cloud to cover his approach until he judged his P-38 to be right on the enemy fighter's tail. Pulling up into the clear he found himself some 200 feet behind and flamed the Bf 110 with a full, accurate burst.

As he pulled up to regain altitude and hopefully link up with his flight, his problems began. His left engine blew up forcing him to feather the propeller and head back down into the cloud. Normally such a power loss would not have been automatically fatal. However, housed within the left boom was the single generator installed on early P-38J-10-LO variants. Now it was a toss-up whether his battery would be drained while powering the fuel cross-feed before he could use all the remaining fuel in the left wing-tanks. The likelihood of running out of fuel before reaching the Dutch coast was a real one but Frey felt he had a chance to gain access to the Dutch Resistance should he be forced to bale out over Holland.

Breaking into clear skies and with ice steadily robbing the ailing P-38 of air speed, he avoided small town by banking right and settled back on course. Just then a succession of flak bursts filled the sly around him; the final shell damaged his intact engine, which started smoking. He soon reasoned that he would have to belly-in or jump. Not wanting to present the Luftwaffe with what was a new P-38 variant, he elected to jump. Pulling swiftly up to 4,000 feet he leveled off and turned over before attempting to drop out, easier said than done because he caught both feet around the control column. A frantic kick soon freed him and he fell away to a safe if lumpy descent into a soggy field

A comic scenario now unfolded. Two of a group of men and women rushed up calling out "Me Frenchman", confusing Frey who surely had doubts about his navigation at this stage. (the French were forced-laborers from that country). Use of his escape language booklet proved inconclusive whereupon he decided to head South. Sighting what he took to be another "French-man" emerging from a house, he again consulted his booklet. His question to the man "Are there any Germans

Ground crewmen attend to a pair of P-38Js. The aircraft at the left was Lieutenant Lewis' *Hells Belles*. Hangar maintenance was a rarity and hangar space was usually reserved for major repair work or conversions.

***Wilma II/Joyce.* a P-38J-15 of the 79th Fighter Squadron, carries full D-Day markings and a White band around the nose section.**

Lieutenant Harry Bisher with his P-38J, *Kitty*, at RAF Wittering. Bisher was declared Missing in Action on 4 March 1944, but evaded capture and returned to England along with Colonel Montomery. The aircraft was lost on 5 May 1944 after a double engine failure.

A crew chief works on the cockpit of this P-38J of the79th Fighter Squadron. There appears to be some damage to the rear of the canopy, which is covered by a trap. The fuselage insignia has been Grayed out (via Larry Davis)

(Left) This P-38J of the 79th Fighter Squadron made a belly landing on return to base. The port engine was feathered prior to landing, while the starboard engine was running at the time of impact and has had the propeller heavily damaged. There is heavy exhaust staining along both booms and on the vertical stabilizers. (via Larry Davis)

This 79th Fighter Squadron P-38J lost power on take off. In the following crash, the aircraft shed both propellers, tore the rudders, and landing gear.

***JEANNE*, a P-38J of the 55th Fighter Squadron carries a scoreboard that includes two locomotives, one patrol boat, one aircraft kill, nine fighter sweeps, two bombing missions, two top cover missions and at least thirtybomber escort missions. (via Larry Davis)**

around?" met with a prompt response, but not one to Frey's advantage. The man slammed both hands down on the pilot's shoulders with enough force to push his feet down into the mud, and his brief bid for freedom was over. Ahead lay the protracted journey via Stalag Luft to Stalag Luft I, Barth. A sad note to the day was the loss of Lieutenant Jack Taylor (55th Fighter Squadron); he was almost home when he spun-in near Sutton Bridge.

The steady rate of pilot-losses was to shoot to a shocking level next day when Lieutenant Colonel Montgomery led forty-eight aircraft on a target and withdrawal cover mission. During the mission several flights were bounced but hit back. Lieutenant Morris added to his total with an Bf 109 and Lieutenant Rader (also 77th Fighter Squadron) hit another whose canopy flew off followed by the pilot. Major Johnson (77th Fighter Squadron) latched onto one of a pair of Bf 109s and knocked him down; he had already fought off two others while covering a B-17 straggler. Captain Meyer and Lieutenant Nichols (both 79th Fighter Squadron) each damaged an Me 410. Those flights which elected to return on the deck shot-up numerous targets.

When heads were counted at Kingscliffe the MIA total was an unbelievable eight pilots. This included the entire 79th Fighter Squadron flight led by Colonel Montgomery as well as two other Squadron pilots Lieutenants Smutko and Orr. Completing the total were Lieutenants Minton and Keathley (77th Fighter Squadron). Only two were KIA (Minton and Lieutenant Cooper) while Montgomery would return to England in June. Lieutenants Hanzo, Sands, Smutko, Orr and Keathley would remain POWs.

Nine days passed before the next mission but when the call came it was quite an occasion for the Eighth Air Force, the start of BIG WEEK. Over the next six days the B-17s and B-24s would range over Germany in a concentrated assault upon the enemy's aircraft production capacity. The 20th Fighter Group was involved in four of the five missions, while completing a fifth on the one day when the bombers were grounded. The human cost would be three pilots MIA but kill figures would rise by ten. The latter figure was almost wholly achieved on 20 February.

In the process of giving penetration and withdrawal cover the following pilots scored; (77th Fighter Squadron) Major Johnson got two Fw

A group of 55th Fighter Squadron pilots pose for a group shot before setting off on a shuttle mission to Russia on 11 September 1944. The arm bands identify the pilot as "friendlies" to any Russian they might come in contact with.

Colonel Harold Rau (Group Commander) steps clear of the cockpit of his P-51D after returning from the FRANTIC IV (shuttle to Russia) mission in September of 1944. The American flag arm band was used to identify the pilot as "friendly" for the Soviets in the event of a bail-out or forced landing.

Lieutenant Dale Jones (79th Fighter Squadron) and his father, who was assigned to a B-26 Group) pose with *Nina Merle II*. The aircraft carried a checkerboard design between the group marking and the anti-glare panel.

Captain Jack Ilfrey's flight jacket patch was the "Winged 8" of the 8th Air Force along with his squadron (79th Fighter Squadron) and Group (20th Fighter Group). The aircraft name, Happy Jack's Go Buggy, was given an outline to make it stand out against the Black Group marking.

(Above & Below) A line-up of recently delivered P-51Ds. The group transitioned to the Mustang beginning in July of 1944. These aircraft have not had their squadron or individual codes applied, but carry the Black triangle marking of the 55th Fighter Squadron.

190s, Lieutenant Williams one Bf 109 with a second shared with Lieutenant Arthaud. (79th Fighter Squadron) Captains Jackson and Graham each shot down two Fw 190s. In addition damaged claims were entered by Lieutenant Hallberg (55th Fighter Squadron) and Lieutenants Williams and Gese (also 77th Fighter Squadron). The overall sense of joy with these results must have been somewhat marred by the absence

(L-R) Captain Slanker, Major Price and Major Gatterdam pose beside a group Mustang. Slanker served as the 77th Fighter Squadron Assistant Operations Officer and Assistant Group Operations Officer. Gatterdam flew one tour as a 79th Fighter Squadron flight leader then flew a second tour as the 55th Fighter Squadron Commander. The three pilots together flew a total of 806 combat hours.

LC-X was flown by Captain Huey of the 77th Fighter Squadron. The aircraft carried two names, *MAGGIE* and *SANDY*. Sandy was the name of Captain Huey's crew chief's, T/SGT Bartram, wife.

This P-51D Mustang of the 79th Fighter Squadron has the early style Black and White nose markings and has been camouflaged along the upper surfaces. The aircraft was named *"Jackie"*. (via Larry Davis)

of Captain Jackson, although he was later confirmed as a POW in Barth.

The 21 and 22 February missions were quiet by comparison. A misdirected return route over the Ruhr on the 22nd (which involved the Group being recalled beyond Munster) introduced the pilots to well-directed flak patterns. Lieutenant Geiger, finding himself separated from the others while taking evasive action, dived for the deck. Among targets strafed by him was an Italian Cant Z506 float-plane; in destroying it he almost shared its fate by striking tree branches with his wing. He came home, but his lease on freedom had a bare forty-eight hours to run. A familiarization sweep over the Dutch coast (23 February) was completely ignored by the defenses. The next day, while taking the 1st Bomb Division to Schweinfurt, the group's sole kill was achieved by Lieutenant Morris who chased and destroyed a Bf 110. On the return leg Lieutenants Geiger and Quiring (55th Fighter Squadron) disappeared. Geiger became a POW but there was no such reprieve for Quiring, who was listed as KIA.

The final BIG WEEK run to Regensburg was incident-free apart from Lieutenant Lauren Taylor who came home on one engine; exactly one month later he would be killed in a crash at Kingscliffe.

On 28 February, the Group went on a short-haul run to Northern France, the only incident being the forced-landing when the landing gear failed on Lieutenant Lewis' (79th Fighter Squadron) Lightning. Flying with the Group on 29 February was Colonel Grambo (364th Fighter Group). Returning from Brunswick with one engine out, he was over the Zuiderzee when the other caught fire so forcing his bale-out. His death was later confirmed, probably due to falling in the frigid water, where he drowned or died of exposure. Lieutenant Bob Johnson (77th Fighter Squadron) was down to one good engine as he crossed out but soon after announcing that he was turning back the other was began to run rough; a POW berth at Barth was his ultimate fate.

BIG WEEK was succeeded in March by "BIG B". This was the expression among 8th Air Force personnel for Berlin. Not only was it the Nazi Capital, but it housed many important industrial plants worthy of attack. It would be effectively struck four times in March, but the initial attack was planned, launched and largely aborted twice.

The 20th Fighter Group would be in the vanguard of the 8th Fighter Command's efforts to protect the "Big Friends" from what was expected to be one of the, if not the, fiercest Luftwaffe reaction to such incur-

Major Jack Ilfrey and his crew pose with his P-51D *HAPPY JACK'S GO BUGGY*. The aircraft has a total of six kills on the fuselage side just below the windscreen. (via Larry Davis)

A flight of Mustangs from the 77th Fighter Squadron with reduced D-Day stripes. Aircraft K and S were both delivered during September of 1944 and both were lost on 19 February 1945. K was flown by Lieutenant Murrell. LC-S survived the war and was scrapped in September of 1945.

Lieutenant Colonel Montomery has just completed a mission and was still in his flight gear. Major Gustke (77th Fighter Squadron Commander) is on the right and Colonel Rau is on the left. The other officer is unidentified.

Lieutenant Ed Pogue flew this P-51D named *Chattanooga Choo Choo*. The bar under the R indicated that this was the second MC R in the squadron. Pogue's final score was six destroyed and three damaged, all ground attack kills.

(Right) Major Jack Price hold up his choice for in a Lockheed "Pin-up" girl contest. He originally served with the 78th Fighter Group (P-47s and P-51s) prior to his assignment in February of 1945 as 55th Fighter Squadron Commander. He later became the Deputy Group Commander.

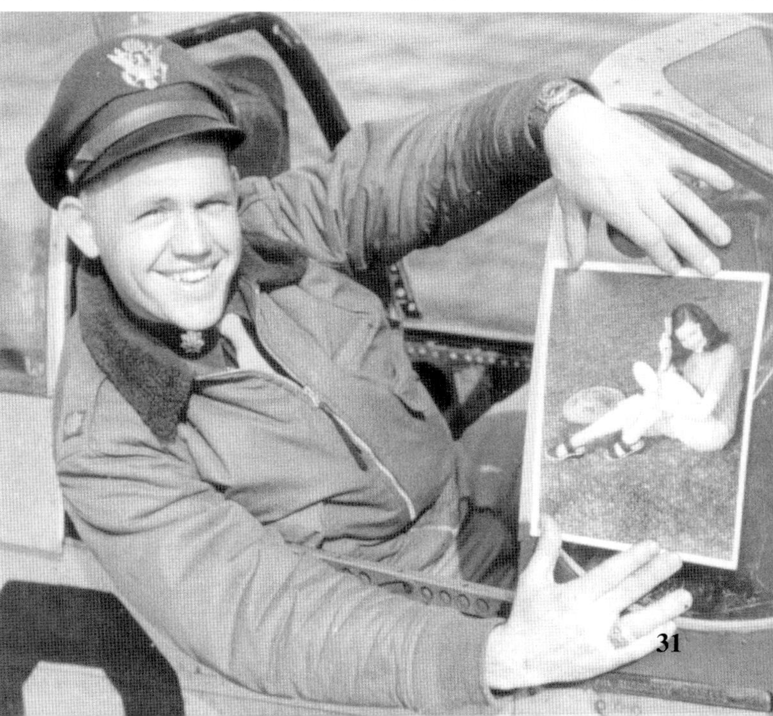

Lieutenant Ernst Fiebelkorn flew this P-51D, *June Nite*, named for his wife. His large size (6 foot 4 inches) made it difficult for him to fit in the small cockpit of the P-51. He was an Ace with eleven kills on the canopy frame.

sions. March, however, began on a deceptive note when medium altitude patrols were mounted to intercept fighters attempting to hit the 3rd Bomb Division B-17s bombing Chartres airfield. The next day (3 March) saw the first abortive run to Berlin. Briefed for withdrawal cover, aborts cut the original forty-eight aircraft formation by ten as the P-38s forged a path through deteriorating weather conditions to Leipzig. Finding no bomber force, Lieutenant Colonel Hubbard (appointed Group Commander in place of Colonel Russell who had gone to Headquarters 8th Fighter Command) took the Group home. Only thirty-seven aircraft returned with Lieutenant Goble (55th Fighter Squadron) having turned South at the Dutch coast. Hopes he might have got down safely were dashed by confirmation of his death.

Berlin next day was again abortive for all but two 3rd Bomb Division Bomb Groups. The 20th Fighter Group was assigned the same region, but again returned having found nothing to escort. Despite no combat action, three pilots were MIA, all 55th Fighter Squadron personnel. Scott disappeared on the way in a suspected victim of anoxia (oxygen starvation) and his remains were never found. He become one of sixteen Group pilots whose names are commemorated on "Wall of the Missing" tablets at various U. S. Military Cemeteries across Europe. Lieutenant Pfeiffer suffered accumulative engine failure which forced him to jump into captivity. Lieutenant Harry Bisher suffered a power loss and was out over the North Sea before he turned back. Gliding down with both engines dead he was intercepted by Lieutenant Gerd Weigand, a JG26 Ace flying an Fw 190. His attempt to persuade the American to direct his P-38 towards a nearby Luftwaffe field were responded to by Bisher easing his nose round to sight his guns on his adversary. Veering hastily away, Weigand came in again and shot the P-38 down with Bisher happily baling out. Now began a four month spell of evasion and a safe return to England during which time he met up with Colonel Montgomery, both regaining friendly soil simultaneously. This mission was nearly the final one for Lieutenant Fogg (79th Fighter Squadron). First, he was fired upon by a P-47 which he evaded by diving into the clouds. When he came over Spanhoe airfield North of Kingscliffe he was already on one engine and further trouble now struck because his right main-gear would not descend. Pulling up for another circuit, his good engine now quit and he came down in an opencast coal-mine. The

P-51s of the 55th Fighter Squadron on the grass at Kingscliffe. The aircraft in the foreground, *JEANNIE* (assigned to Lieutenant Pannell) is an early P-51D without the fin fillet. The aircraft was later lost while being flown by Captain Taylor on 19 October 1944. The pilot successfully bailed out, was captured and became a POW.

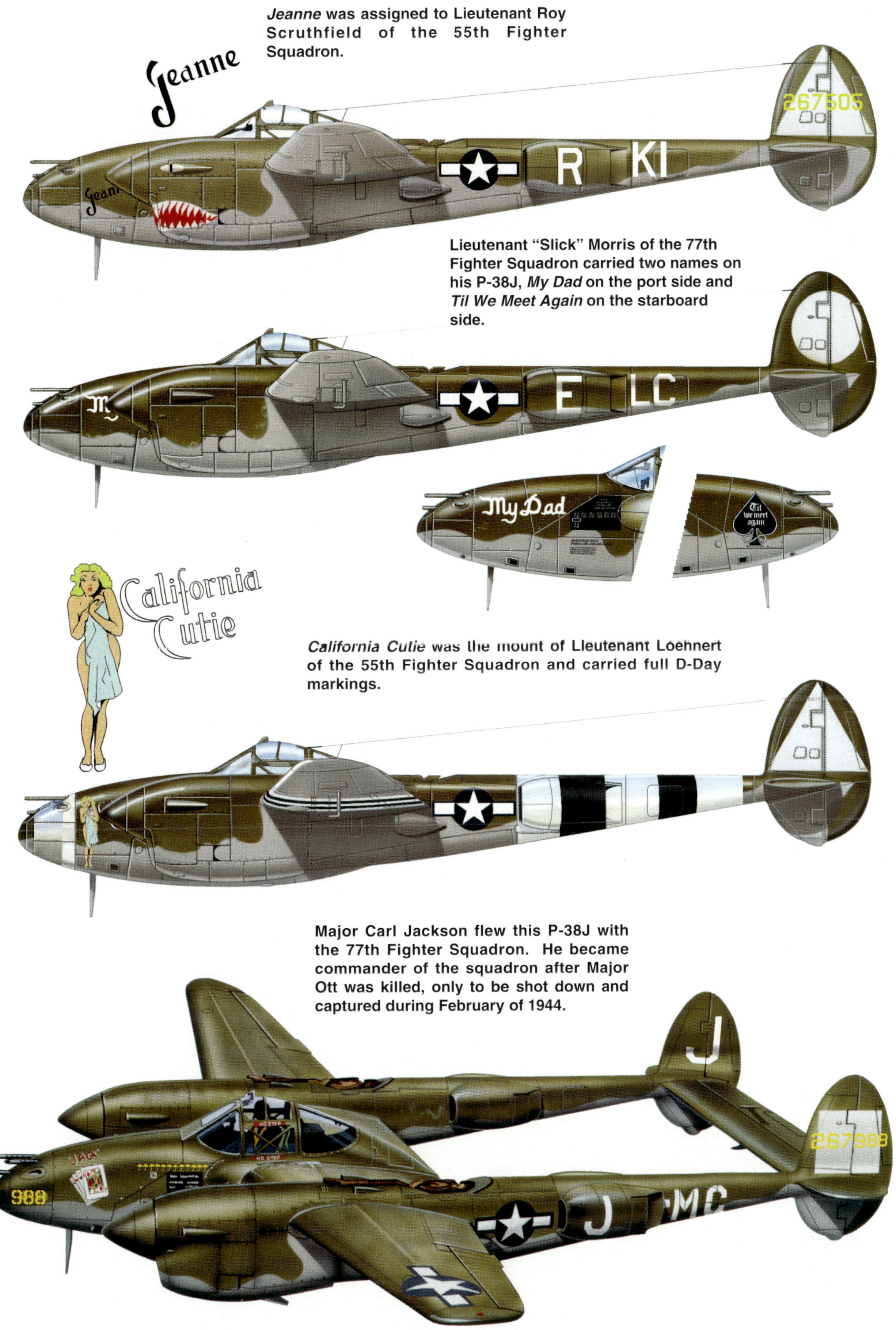

Jeanne was assigned to Lieutenant Roy Scruthfield of the 55th Fighter Squadron.

Lieutenant "Slick" Morris of the 77th Fighter Squadron carried two names on his P-38J, *My Dad* on the port side and *Til We Meet Again* on the starboard side.

California Cutie was the mount of Lieutenant Loehnert of the 55th Fighter Squadron and carried full D-Day markings.

Major Carl Jackson flew this P-38J with the 77th Fighter Squadron. He became commander of the squadron after Major Ott was killed, only to be shot down and captured during February of 1944.

A flight of four P-51s of the 77th Fighter Squaron peel off for landing. The three aircraft in the background are P-51Ds, while the aircraft in the foreground is a P-51B, *PATS PONY*, flown by Lieutenant J. MacAuthor.

aircraft caught fire and his left foot was trapped by the controls, putting him into a grave situation. Personnel from the 318th Transport Carrier Group on the base fought the blaze while a Flight Surgeon cut off Fogg's shoe where upon he was hauled out (the array of instruments pulled out by the surgeon convinced Fogg that one definite option for extracting him was to cut off his foot or lower leg, instead of just his shoe). He would enjoy another eight weeks at Kingscliffe before he exchanged its comfort for the even more Spartan conditions in Stalag Luft III.

Although resistance to the forces attacking Berlin on 6, 8 and 9 March was severe, at least on the first two missions, the 20th Fighter Group witnessed little action apart from the first, when Lieutenant Yelton scored against a Bf 109. Otherwise the duties of general escort were carried out faultlessly. The abort rate was minimal, although it rose to eight over Brunswick (15 March). Targets in SW Germany on 16 March were similarly void of combat but flak accounted for Lieutenant Matyasz (55th Fighter Squadron) over Belgium, an action he did not survive.

Lieutenant Colonel Hubbard had commanded the Group for a mere fifteen days when he set off for Augsberg/Oberpfaffenhofen (18 March). On this occasion he handed overall command to Major Franklin. Escort duties from St Dizier to Ulm were carried out and the P-38s were duly relieved by P-51s. South of Ulm the 79th Fighter Squadron saw three Bf 110s taking off and White and Red Flights dived on them with

A very weathered P-51D of the 55th Fighter Squadron taxies in after a mission. There is battle damage under the horizontal stabilizer and the fuselage national insignia has been "Grayed out."

Lieutenant Harley Brown of the 55th fighter Squadron shakes hands with one of his ground crew. His aircraft, *Be Good*, carries seven kill markings on the fuselage under the cockpit. The aircraft also carried the name *BROWNIES BALLROOM* on the canopy rail.

Yellow Flight covering. Major Franklin clobbered one, which blew up while Captain Nichols headed after the second. The German pilot maneuvered his fighter in a manner which caused Nichols to miss on his first pass but after two further passes ended the German fighter exploded. Captain Graham and Lieutenant Heiden also required two passes to bring down the last Bf 110. It crash landed with the crew hastily evacuating the wreck. Stark tragedy now ensued as Graham came in on a strafing run. Heiden saw him strike the ground, pull up in a barrel-roll and while still inverted smash into the snow-covered ground. A veteran of many air battles in the past three months, Graham was also one of the first Group Aces. Whether he suffered some form of white-out and accordingly mis-judged his height would never be known, but his loss was a particularly severe one for his Squadron and the 20th Fighter Group.

Aircraft at Memmingen were spotted by Major McAuley leading the 55th Fighter Squadron. This time Captain Serros (Red Flight Leader) was detached to attack. Serros and Lieutenant Hallberg pursued a Bf 110 as it took off, finally scoring lethal hits. Back with the bombers McAuley's Flight was engaged by two small groups of Bf 109s; the former was driven off while the second was taken on by the Major and his wingman, one being downed by "Mac".

Colonel Hubbard's Flight had become separated from the Group while climbing through the undercast but on reaching the bomber formations immediately attacked some twenty enemy fighters. The battle which developed progressed downward to ground level. In the course of the combat both Hubbard and Lieutenant Clark, his wingman, each knocked down an Bf 109 and shared a third. Now with two more Messerschmitts in pursuit the P-38 duo used their extra power to zoom-climb away before dropping down close to the ground. Unknown to them they were flying right into a flak trap formed by the batteries protecting the huge Messerschmitt complex at Augsburg. Strikes on Hubbard's P-38's left side set it on fire. Being at full throttle and with very uninviting terrain

***ITS THE KID!* of the 77th Fighter Squadron was assigned to Lieutenant Alexander. It has the bars of the national insignia toned down, but the star was left untouched.**

SAD SACK **was Major Gilbertson's regular aircraft. The tip of the spinner was Silver, and the group markings do no extend completely around the lower cowling. There are six kill markings on the canopy rail.**

in which to attempt a crash-landing, Hubbard's only option was to jump. Even this act was none too soon because barely had his chute deployed when he struck the ground hard and awkwardly. He was quickly apprehended by gunners from the flak units.

Once again a trio of personnel losses hit the group. Lieutenant Butler (77th Fighter Squadron) was seen to bale out over the sea off Texel; he remains missing to this day. A fourth pilot, Lieutenant Singleton (McAuley's wingman) was escorting the latter back home, Mac having lost an engine, when he suffered successive engine-loss. Like Lieutenant Butler he also baled out over the sea. Fortunately within a short period he was fished out by an ASR launch. Exposure in the cold water often killed within minutes.

Berlin (22 March) and Brunswick (23 March) were free of incident as was Bordeaux (27 March). The latter mission was the first for Colonel Hubbard's replacement, Colonel Harold Rau. The new man was no desk-jockey having previously commanded the 356th Fighter Group at Martlesham Heath. Apart from making a solid impression among his new subordinates, he would also have two spells in command, up to late June when he returned for States-side leave, resuming command in late August for a further three and a half months.

For the pilots hovering around the B-17s bombing Rheims/Champagne airfield (28 March) little untoward was so far observed. Indeed only two

The crew chief of *Little Lady,* runs an engine test on the aircraft's hardstand during late 1944. The drop tanks in position under the wings suggest that the aircraft was being prepared for an upcoming mission.

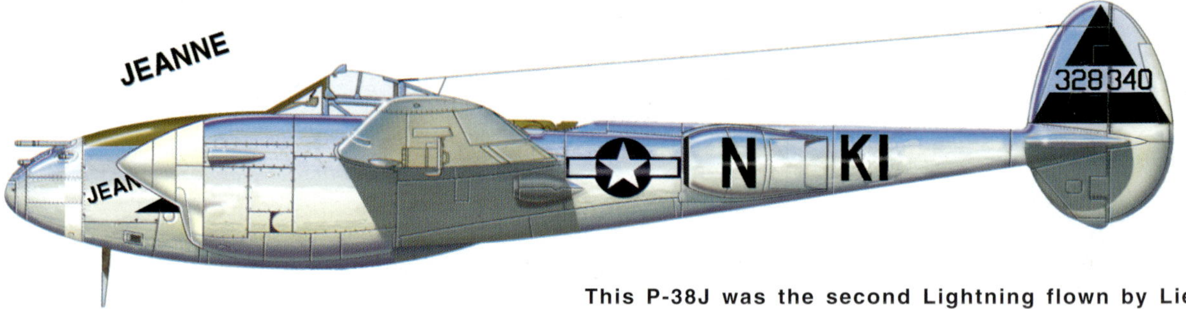

This P-38J was the second Lightning flown by Lieutenant Scrutchfield of the 55th Fighter Squadron to carry the name *JEANNE* (named for his wife).

"Lucky Lady" was a P-38J assigned to Lieutenant Arthur W. Heiden. He completed a total of 300 combat hours in this Lightning.

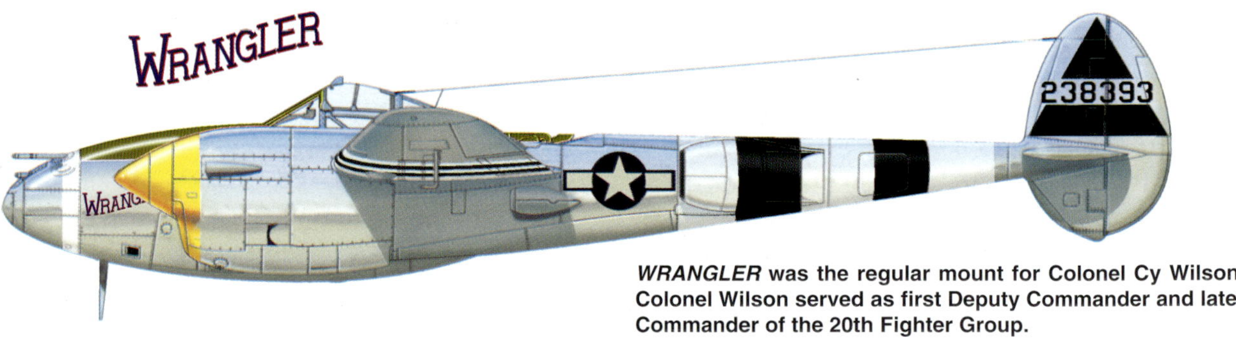

WRANGLER was the regular mount for Colonel Cy Wilson. Colonel Wilson served as first Deputy Commander and later Commander of the 20th Fighter Group.

Colonel Bob Meyers of the 79th Fighter Squadron was the regular pilot of *Bobcat II.* The aircraft was declared MIA while being flown by Lieutenant H. Watson on 25 May 1944.

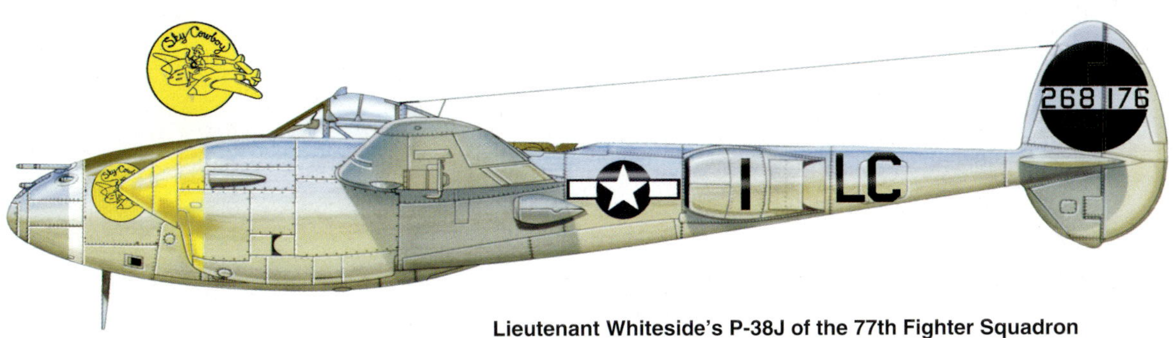

Lieutenant Whiteside's P-38J of the 77th Fighter Squadron was named *Sky Cowboy*. The Lightning was lost in a take off accident on 12 July 1944, while being flown by another pilot.

MAMA'S BOY, a P-38J Lightning of the 55th Fighter Squadron carried full D-Day markings.

Colonel Rau flew this P-38J named *"Gentle Annie"* during his first tour as commander of the 20th Fighter Group. He would later return to the Group and assume command while flying P-51s.

Jack Ilfrey named his P-38J *HAPPY JACK'S GO BUGGY*. At this point in his career he had eight kills and two locomotives to his credit.

***Nina Merle III* carried three kill markings on the canopy rail. The aircraft serial number was partially obscured by the squadron tail marking.**

bombers out of the 264 making effective sorties would be lost. The distinct possibility that a third could have been added to this figure was noted by Lieutenant Hallberg among others. Just after bombs away a 381st Bomb Group Fortress absorbed two devastating flak bursts around its rear fuselage. It spun away down presumably to its inevitable impact with French soil and the loss of some or all of its crew. Surprisingly, the Fortress made a successful recovery many thousands of feet below the departing bomber formations, at which point eight of the P-38s directed themselves towards the straggler. Hallberg closed with the cripple and having noted the bomber's errant course was taking it Southward, he redirected the pilots using sign-language. A safe passage back to England was made and the fighters departed. (After the War Hallberg made contact with the pilot Lieutenant Dan Henry who told him that recovery was made by using the auto-pilot, the main control cables being inoperative until a temporary 'splicing' job was carried out after the B-17 was stabilized. Five of the seven men surviving the blast were baled out over their base (Ridgewell) after which the pilots took their bomber out to the Suffolk coast where it was abandoned to its watery fate.)

The heightened pace of combat for the Eighth was sustained during April. Also, there would be a distinct change in operational activities for the 20th Fighter Group which would bring an upsurge in morale. That change should have been heralded on 5 April when twelve Fighter Groups were briefed to carry out strafing attacks on German airfields. Salzwedel was assigned to the 20th Fighter Group, but heavy cloud caused Colonel Rau to abort. Lieutenant Yelton (55th Fighter Squadron) was last seen near Hanover. In fact, he had sustained an unlucky flak hit while the Group was in the overcast. Recovering much lower down, he discovered his instruments (including the compass) were largely inoperative. With no sun available to point him westward, Yelton had to resort to luck. In the course of his homeward flight he came across an Fw 200 Kondor which was brought down in its airfield pattern. Soon afterwards a Fw 190 was stalked and set on fire with the pilot jumping clear. Engine power was steadily failing to Yelton decided to belly-in on another airfield looming up. On approach he saw two Bf 110s ready for take-off. The tactic of "Kamikaze Attack" was something alien to western minds when applied later in the Second World War by the Japanese. Yelton's final action with his P-38 pre-dated that assault technique by many months; he now headed straight for the Messerschmitts and impacted with them. His subsequent survival, by being thrown clear, albeit with two broken and dislocated shoulders, was

A pair of P-51Ds of the 77th Fighter Squadron in formation over the English country-side during the late Summer of 1944. LC-F is carrying drop tanks, while LC-N has jettisioned his.

CORKY **was assigned to Lieutenant Tom Daniel of the 79th Fighter Squadron. The aircraft arrived in August or September of 1944 and was scrapped in July of 1945. The name was added by Lieutenant Barnard when he took it over.**

a miracle. Equally miraculous was his treatment at the hands of the Luftwaffe personnel who apprehended him; their fury at what was an apparently cold-blooded action which killed all their comrades could easily have boiled over into a fatal beating for Yelton.

The weather on 8 April initially grounded the Group but, by 1400, Colonel Rau was leading on a mission which unbeknown to the pilots, would be a water-shed for Group fortunes. Rau had received permission to strafe airfields around Salzwedel and the 20th Fighter Group would be the sole unit to carry out such duties this day. Two airfields North and South of Salzwedel were assigned the 79th Fighter Squadron and 77th Fighter Squadron respectively. The former Squadron was descending on its target when, unluckily for its crew, an He 177 was sighted by Major Franklin; he and four other pilots sent the bomber down to explode on impact. Meanwhile, Colonel Rau and the other pilots were shooting up the airfield to great effect, a total of thirteen aircraft being credited as destroyed.

Soon after leaving the airfield, and while strafing a Wehrmacht barracks where many casualties among the soldiers occurred, the Squadron was bounced. Lieutenant Esau was downed in this attack but managed to bale out. A climbing turn by Rau's Flight brought the Colonel neatly in behind a Bf 109 and his bullets hit home. Sadly the enemy fighter was in a climb and with its pilot probably dead or injured it careened into Lieutenant Snow of Major Franklin's Flight. No parachutes were seen to emerge from the entangled and flaming wreckage. In the meantime Franklin and Lieutenant Lefevre had successfully taken on two more Messerschmitts. To add to the general destruction Rau and Franklin combined to blow up two locomotives passing each other at the time.

The 77th Fighter Squadron were similarly indulging themselves over their airfield where eight aircraft were destroyed. In addition Major Johnson attacked an unidentified twin-engined aircraft landing and watched it crash. Lieutenant Horne swung onto the tail of an Fw 190 approaching head-on and set it on fire.

The ground defenses were handing out punishment as well. Captain Machen's P-38 was fatally crippled and his desperate attempt to bale out failed when his aircraft smashed into the trees. His more fortunate col-

A trio of 79th Fighter Squdron Mustangs. The aircraft in the foreground and far background are both P-51Bs while the aircraft in the middle is a P-51D. The lead P-51B is *Shoot You're Faded*, which was belly-landed at Munich Air Field by Lieutenant Barnard on 21 August 1945.

This Mustang is an early model P-51D without a fin fillet. Lieutenant "Moon" Mullins was flying this aircraft on a local flight on 18 October 1944 when he suffered a fatal crash into the North Sea.

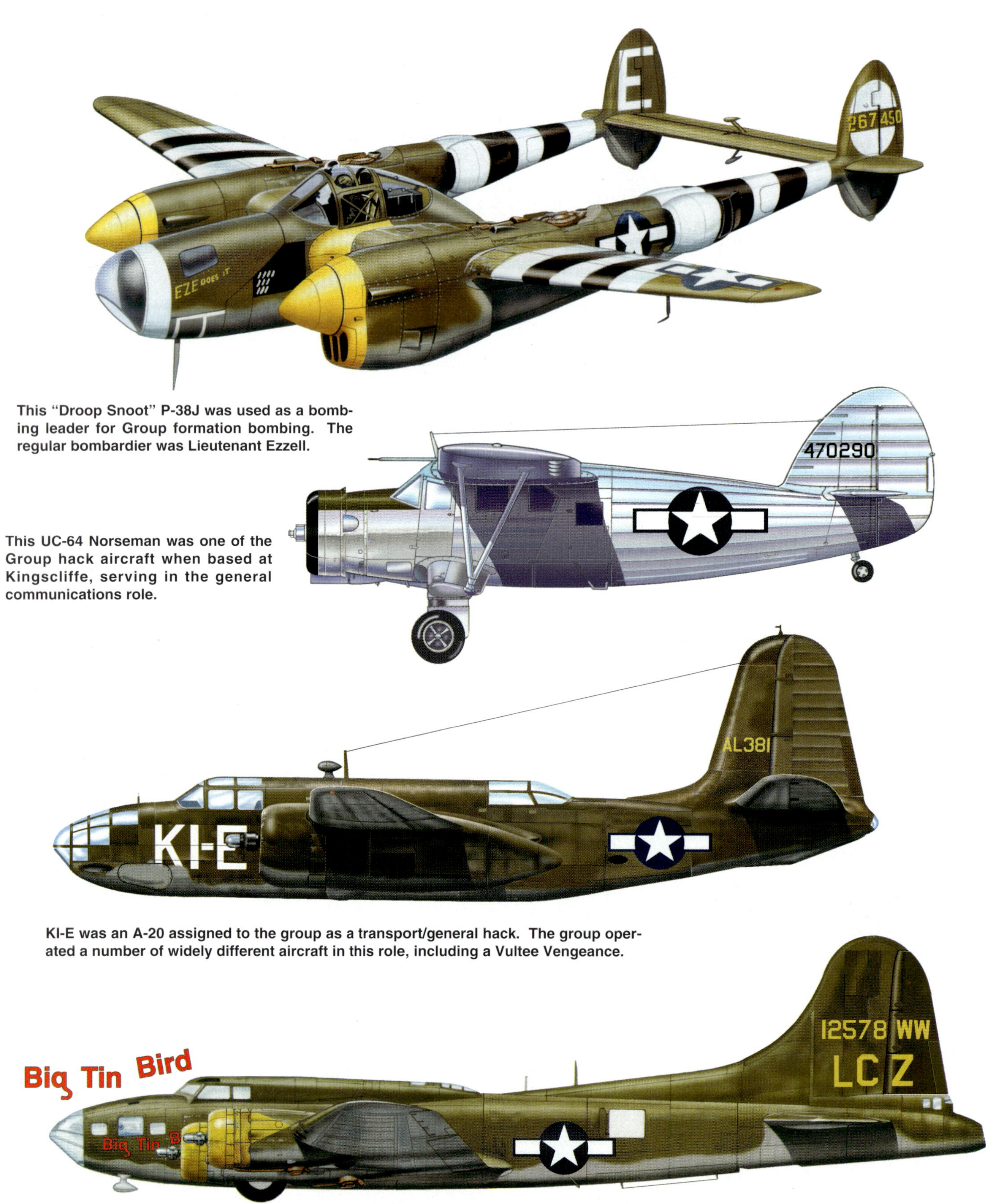

This "Droop Snoot" P-38J was used as a bombing leader for Group formation bombing. The regular bombardier was Lieutenant Ezzell.

This UC-64 Norseman was one of the Group hack aircraft when based at Kingscliffe, serving in the general communications role.

KI-E was an A-20 assigned to the group as a transport/general hack. The group operated a number of widely different aircraft in this role, including a Vultee Vengeance.

Big Tin Bird was a B-17E Flying Fortress that was declared "War Weary," stripped of its armament and assigned to the Group as a transport late in the war.

This 77th Fighter Squadron Mustang was assigned to Lieutenant Alexander but was being flown by Lieutenant Kennedy when he was declared Missing In Action (MIA) on 2 November 1944.

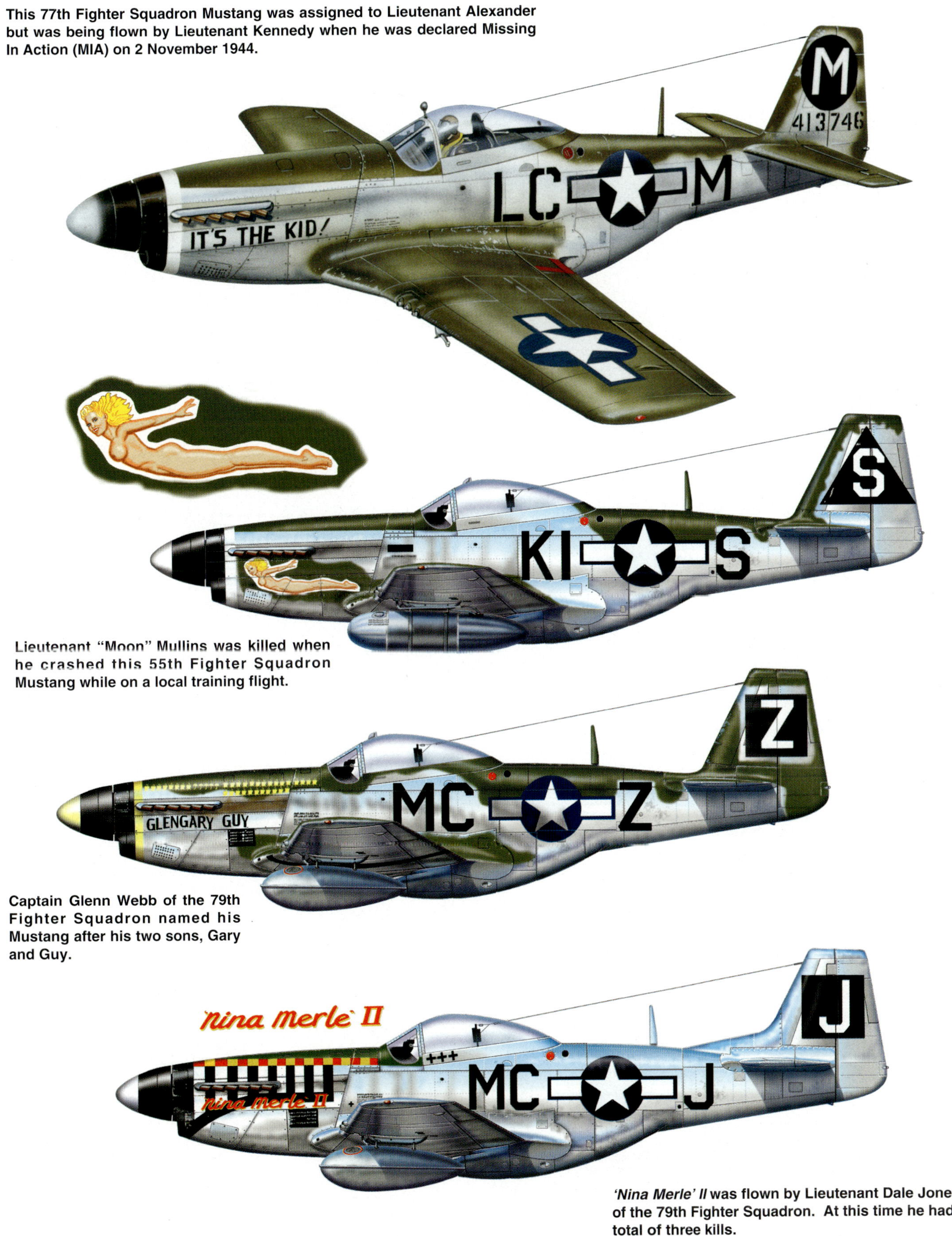

Lieutenant "Moon" Mullins was killed when he crashed this 55th Fighter Squadron Mustang while on a local training flight.

Captain Glenn Webb of the 79th Fighter Squadron named his Mustang after his two sons, Gary and Guy.

'Nina Merle' II was flown by Lieutenant Dale Jones of the 79th Fighter Squadron. At this time he had a total of three kills.

Mustangs of the 55th Fighter Squadron taxi out for another mission during the late Summer of 1944. The aircraft carry camouflage on their upper surfaces. KI-O was named *Mama's Boy* and was flown by Lieutenant Ed Wasil.

leagues continued to strafe available targets which included another locomotive busted by Lieutenant Morris.

The 55th Fighter Squadron had no assigned targets and contented themselves with hitting oil-dumps, factories, flak positions and any other suitable facility, including locomotives, of which eight were thoroughly "punctured". The unit's "Loco-busters" reputation was now firmly established. On the down-side, there were three losses, with Lieutenant Singleton joining Snow and Machen on the MIA list; in his case he survived.

It would be some days before strafing would be a standard briefed feature of missions. Two days after Salzwedel another assault variation was practiced for the first time. Precision bombing had hitherto been the monopoly of the B-17s, B-24s and B-26s. Fighter-bombers had usually resorted to dive-bombing, this being the only method of sighting on the target for their pilots. A variant of the P-38 incorporating a clear nose cap and carrying a bombardier in place of the gun-bay was now in service. Using one of these as a Lead Ship the remaining P-38s could fly in formation carrying 500 pound or 1,000 pound bombs. This refined concept of the fighter-bomber permitted a sizable concentration of bombs on the target, apart from which the P-38s could traverse the bomb- run at a more comfortable speed than their less fortunate colleagues in the heavies. In turn, the P-38 pilots gained even more respect for the bomber crews as they now faced the pressure of holding formation in the face of sometimes heavy flak, no evasive action was allowed on these runs.

The day prior to the first bombing mission (9 April) the Group had flown a wearying mission to Tutow, Poland during which, for the second time a visiting pilot, Lieutenant Dettre of the 474th Fighter Group,

E K and Jay Bee/Suzanne was assigned to Lieutenant J. B. Lee during October of 1944. She was the second P-51 to carry the code MC-L. The Mustang survived the war and was scrapped during March of 1946.

***"Frisco Belle"* was the personal mount of Captain Cosgriff of the 55th Fighter Squadron.**

Captain Chet Jennings poses with his Mustang named *Jean* (for his wife). He served in the group between August of 1944 and the war's end. The last four number of the serial are painted on the landing gear door in Black.

A pair of P-51Bs of the 55th Fighter Squadron with the same identification letter, Q. The aircraft at the right has a fin fillet while the aircraft in the foreground is a standard P-51B without the fillet.

failed to return. On 10 April, the specialist P-38 known as a Droop-snoot led the bomb-laden Lightning formation to Florennes airfield. The Bombardier was Lieutenant Ezzell, who had completed a tour with the 306th Bomb Group. Bad weather, however, forced an abort and bomb-jettison in the Channel. The resultant good bomb pattern augured well for future missions.

Later in the day an airfield at Gutersloh was struck with good results but at the cost of Major Don Willis (67th Fighter Wing and a veteran of both the RAF and USAF). Fuel pressure problems finally forced him to belly-in. Three consecutive daily runs to Oschersleben and Schweinfurt (twice) produced no action as did the fighter-sweep planned for 18 April, in this instance a weather-front over Holland forced a recall as the Group headed for the area between Bremen and Hanover.

The Oranienburg mission (18 April) was free of combat although enemy fighters tried to draw off the P-38s by hovering on the flanks and above the bomber stream.

On the homeward leg and while still over the North Sea, Lieutenant Henslee (55th Fighter Squadron) elected to bale out; he had previously lost one engine which reportedly dislodged from its mounting. Four pilots circled him while waiting the ASR Service launch but Henslee was never picked up, the North Sea swallowed him up as it had so many other airmen.

Two more incident free missions were followed on 22 April by a combined escort/strafing brief in which the 79th Fighter Squadron stayed all the way with the bombers and the other Squadrons strafed in the Hamm to Koblenz zone.

The second completed Droop-snoot run was made next day against an Fw repair plant at Tours and also Chateaudun airfield. The majority of the Group attacked the former target and joining in the strafing of the latter after bombs away. Good concentrations were reported at each location, but flak again extracted a price with two 55th Fighter Squadron aircraft downed. Major McAuley, who had assumed Squadron command from Major Clark on 18 March, was forced to bale out but was seen to wave as he floated down. German reports were to state that "Mac" subsequently died from wounds received in the air. Another fine leader noted for his calm but firm control was gone. The other pilot shot down was Lieutenant Ahren who shared Mac's fate. Ground-strafing was described by one anonymous pilot as akin to "riding the winner of the Kentucky Derby through a snake-infested swamp." In addition to the risk of being blown out of the sky there was a higher risk of power-loss in the event of the engines suffering coolant leaks from flak hits, a factor not affecting the air-cooled P-47 engines.

Lieutenant "Lucky" Lowman's luck nearly ran out on this landing during the Summer of 1945. The starboard main mount failed on touch down and the aircraft lost the propeller during the crash landing.

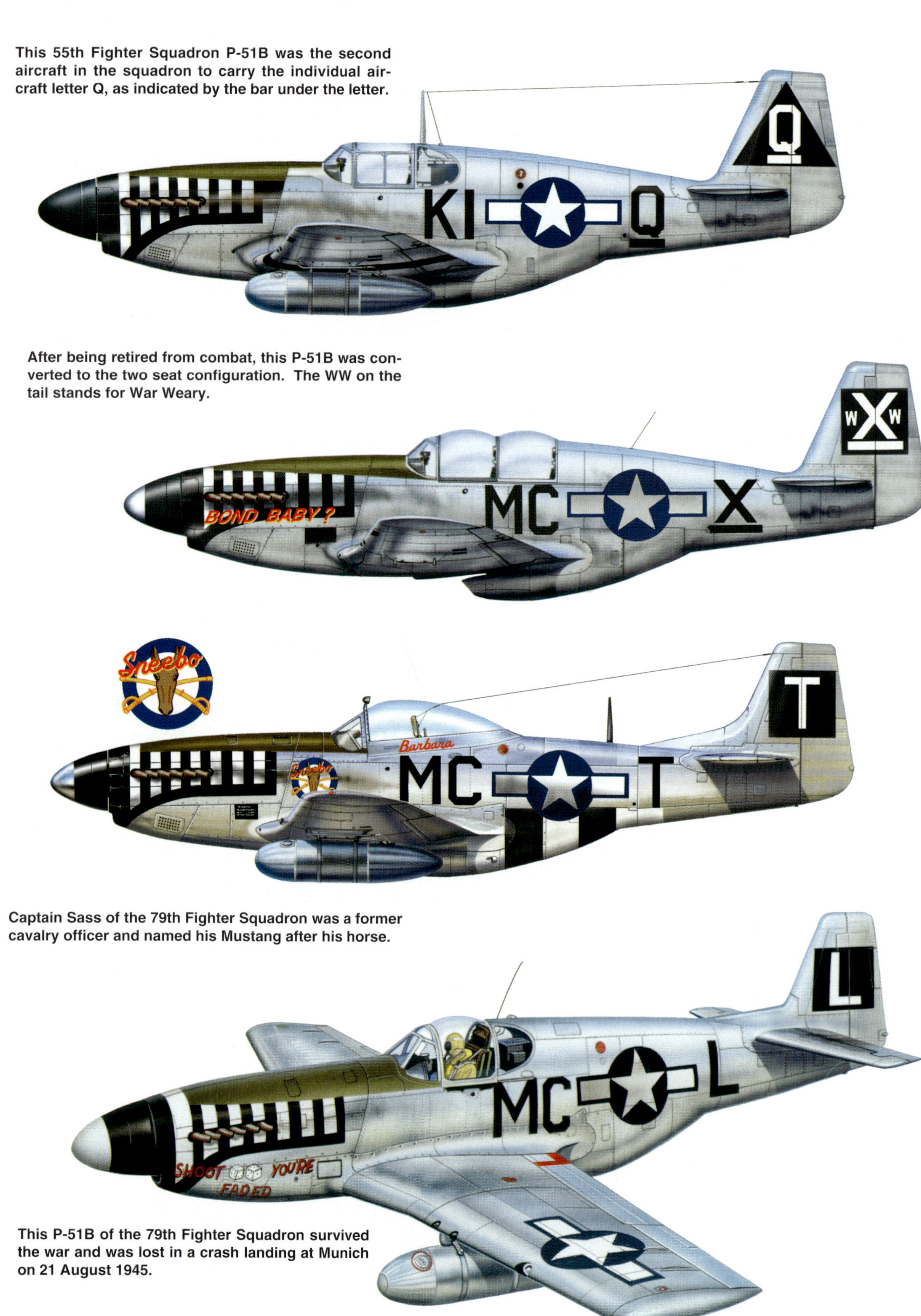

This 55th Fighter Squadron P-51B was the second aircraft in the squadron to carry the individual aircraft letter Q, as indicated by the bar under the letter.

After being retired from combat, this P-51B was converted to the two seat configuration. The WW on the tail stands for War Weary.

Captain Sass of the 79th Fighter Squadron was a former cavalry officer and named his Mustang after his horse.

This P-51B of the 79th Fighter Squadron survived the war and was lost in a crash landing at Munich on 21 August 1945.

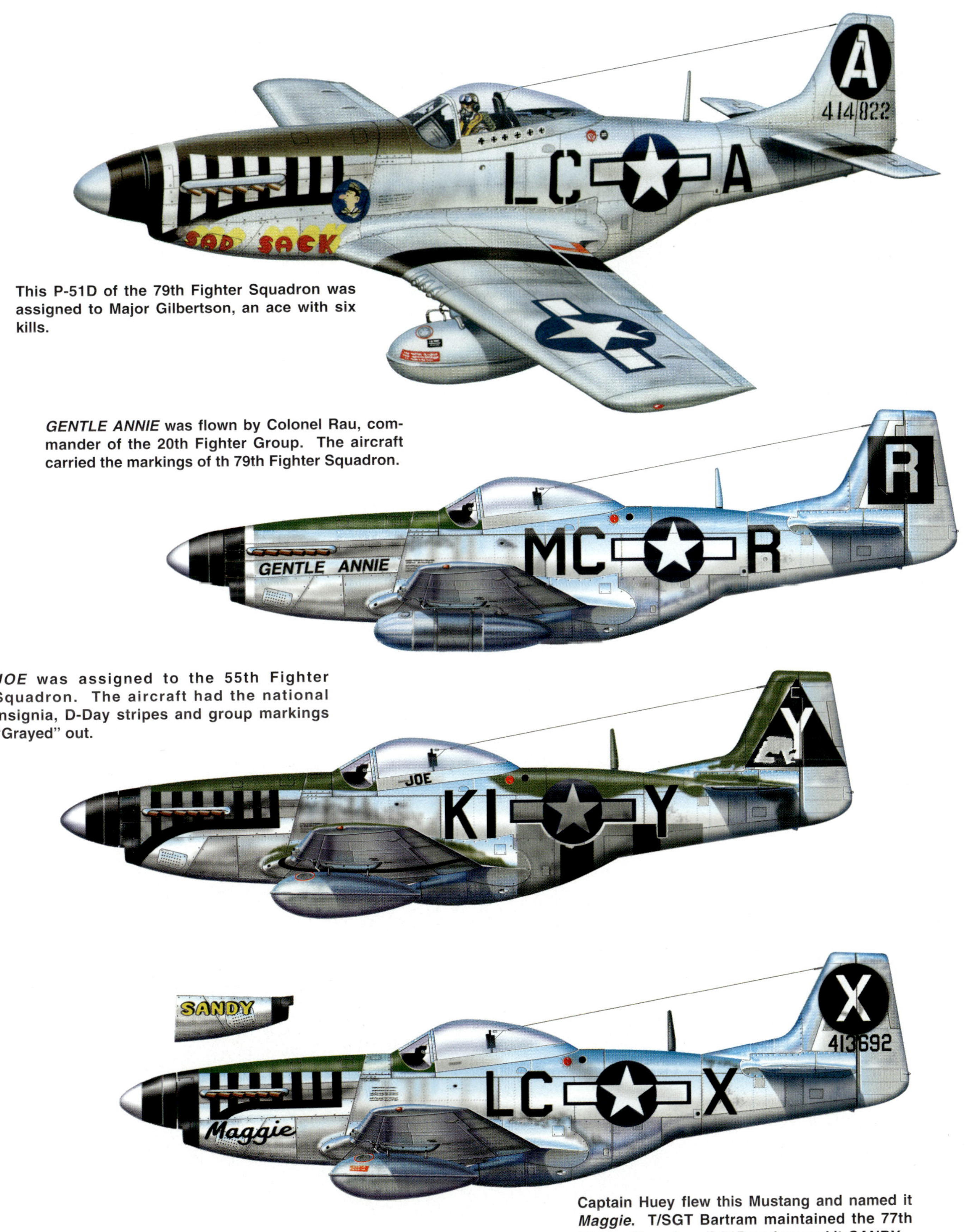

This P-51D of the 79th Fighter Squadron was assigned to Major Gilbertson, an ace with six kills.

GENTLE ANNIE was flown by Colonel Rau, commander of the 20th Fighter Group. The aircraft carried the markings of th 79th Fighter Squadron.

JOE was assigned to the 55th Fighter Squadron. The aircraft had the national insignia, D-Day stripes and group markings "Grayed" out.

Captain Huey flew this Mustang and named it *Maggie*. T/SGT Bartram maintained the 77th Fighter Squadron P-51D and named it *SANDY.*

Captain Sass flew this P-51D named *SNEEBO*. The aircraft has reduced D-Day markings and is carrying pressed paper underwing drop tanks. The aircraft was named for Captain Sass' horse he rode while with the U.S. Cavalry.

The Tours mission heralded daily sorties for the rest of April. A B-24 attack on Gablingen was covered both directions, but on withdrawal, the 55th Fighter Squadron and 77th Fighter Squadron carried out widespread strafing. The former Squadron spotting some Bf 109s over an airfield which were bounced. Two fell to Major Taylor and Lieutenant Watson while Lieutenant Schultz harried a third taking off into a belly-landing; it was then strafed to destruction by Captain Reihmer (77th Fighter Squadron). A total of four destroyed and three damaged locomotives were added to the Group's score.

Visits to Mannheim and Brunswick preceded the third Droop-snoot attack (27 April). The briefed target at Peronne airfield being weather-bound, the P-38s switched to Meaulte airfield. A quarter of the forty-eight aircraft had been briefed to dive-bomb, the rest acting as top cover. The main formation dropped its ordnance but the top cover P-38s were still acting in that capacity when bogies were called in, forcing them to jettison their bombs. The bogies turned out to be P-47s whose aircraft identification seems to have been indifferent to say the least considering the P-38's distinctive outline. The morning sortie was succeeded by an afternoon escort run for B-24s bombing Chalons-Sur-Marne marshaling yards, all part of the steady process of isolating the Normandy region prior to D-Day. Two more Droop-snoot missions were flown on either side of an escort run, closing off April. Tours repair-plant was hit again with one fatal loss; Lieutenant Lefevre spun down after flak hit his aircraft. He was seen to recover but in fact did crash to his death. Berlin (29 April) saw the Group giving cover to the 3rd Bomb Division. As the Rendezvous Point was approached, a call for support from one group sent the fighters to their aid. Some fifty enemy fighters were attacking with an estimated fifty hovering above. The 20th Fighter Group interposed themselves between the bombers and this second force. Over the

Captain Sass crash landed his P-51 *SNEEBO*, when the landing gear failed on touch down. The Black stripes on the wing are probably aiming lines to assist in bombing attacks, The aircraft name and nose art were carried on the port side only.

Sergeant Ed Beck extracts the center propeller hub, watched by his fellow 55th Fighter Squadron maintenance mechanic Sergeant Ken Smith. The Mustang was KI-Z, serial 43-25028.

next twenty minutes individual enemy pilots tried to bounce the bombers but were warded off. Actual contact was minimal but Captain Reihmer did damage one. One opponent succeeded in landing strikes on Lieutenant Fiebelkorn's P-38 but without result. This would be unfortunate for the future well-being of a number of Luftwaffe pilots in the months to come as the Lieutenant ran up a flaming score of air and ground kills to head the Group list of Aces by the War's end.

A duo of Droop-snoot missions (30 April) went out against Tours and Orleans/Bricy airfield with the latter being strafed on both occasions. Flak over Tours accounted for Lieutenant Fogg but at least he became a POW. Lieutenant Klatt (79th Fighter Squadron) was nearly "bombed" out of the sky when a preceding aircraft's weapon struck his right engine nacelle. Lieutenant Panel (55th Fighter Squadron) flew through debris thrown up by a P-47's bomb strike, but managed to return safely.

The May missions largely reflected the Group's primary function as a high-level escort unit. Toward the end of the month, however, the pilots would be more regularly released to carry out strafing attacks once having completed their escort duties. On 1 May, after a short-range escort to Brussels, the pilots went down to hit an airfield south of Liege. This attack was made at a dear cost because Lieutenant Pearson succumbed to flak and was killed while his 55th Fighter Squadron colleague, Lieutenant Schultz was last seen over the field. He was later reported as KIA.

Three missions later, over Brunswick (8 May), the latest Group casualty was suffered when Lieutenant Connor (55th Fighter Squadron) called

This Gloster Meteor Mk III jet fighter of No 226 Operational Conversion Unit visited Kingscliffe and reportedly was flown by several 20th Fighter Group pilots.

Lieutenant John Lundin (left) and Lieutenant Jack Taylor dressed in Class A uniform visit Stamford Village. Both were Killed In Action (KIA) on 10 February 1944.

Staff Sergeant Harry Linden in the cockpit of a P-51B Mustang. With the two section folding canopy, bailing out of an early Mustang could be a problem.

Jack Ilfrey perched on the wing of his P-51D named *HAPPY JACK'S GO BUGGY*. The aircraft carried a total of eight kills at this time. (via Jim Roeder)

Captain William A. Cameron with his ground crew, Tech Sergeant Stanley Lecznar (left) and Corporal John C. Henderson (R) along side his P-51D *SOAR LASSIE II* (MC-C, serial 44-13846).

(Left) Captain Glen Webb of the 79th Fighter Squadron poses with his P-51D Mustang, *GLENGARY GUY* during September of 1944. Webb had two sons, Gary and Guy, which explains the aircraft's name. He completed a total of 362 combat hours during November of 1944 with a score of one Bf 109 destroyed and another claimed as damaged.

With a belt of .50 caliber machine gun ammunition over his shoulder, Staff Sergeant Barlow poses with Colonel Cy Wilson's P-38J *WRANGLER*. His scoreboard carries one kill, twenty-six escort missions, ten top cover missions, seven bombing missions and five fighter sweeps.

A 79th Fighter Squadron P-51D taxies past the Group's UC-64 Norseman "hack". The aircraft was overall Silver with an Olive Drab anti-glare panel and Black cowling ring.

Two of the Group's early commanders. Colonel Barton M. Russel (right) assumed command on 16 January 1943 and brought the Group to England. Ira C. Eaker (left) commanded the group from 16 January to 22 September 1941. He later rose to the rank of General and commanded the 8th U.S. Army Air Force in England until late 1943.

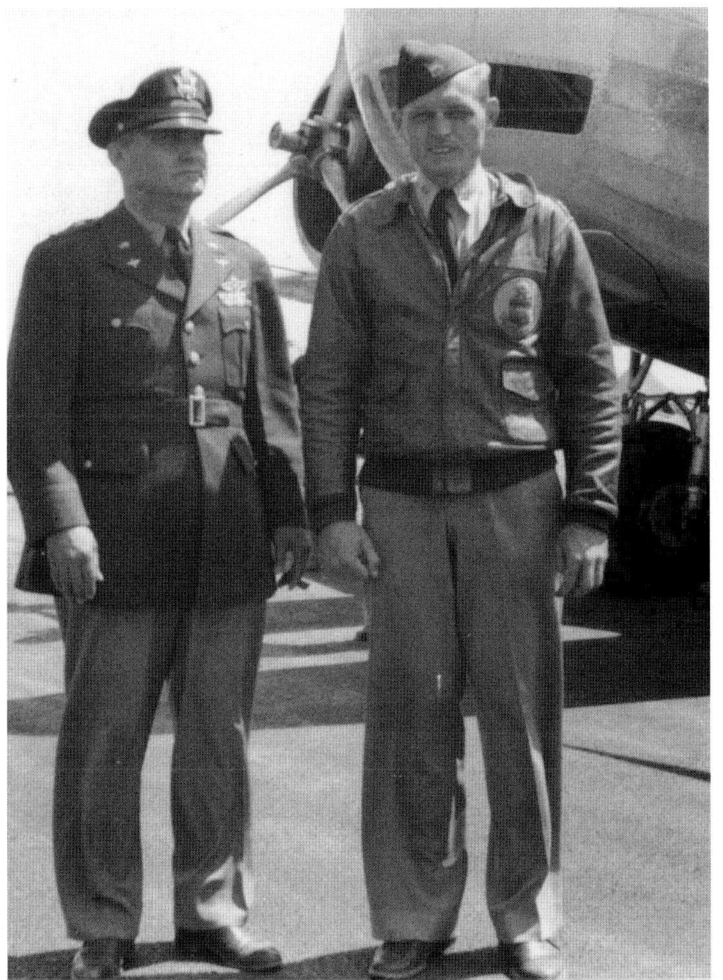

in to say he was baling out, but for reasons unknown he did not survive. Lieutenant McCarty had better luck when his landing-gear would not lower and he had to force land. That good fortune deserted him within twenty-four hours. Departing Luxemboung City the Group was bounced by six Bf 109s, one of which struck McCarty's left boom setting it on fire; the 79th Fighter Squadron pilot baled out into captivity.

Another water-shed in the Combined Bombing Offensive occurred on 12 May, one which would have terminal consequences for Nazi industrial output. Previous attempts to hit bottle neck targets such as ball-bearing plants had failed. Germany, however, depended as much, if not more, upon synthetic oil production to sustain its war effort. Neutralization of these plants would almost certainly create a fatal vacuum in supplies, especially within the Luftwaffe, which depended upon huge quantities to operate.

Covering the 1st Bomb Division on withdrawal from Lutzkendorf's refineries, over thirty Bf 109s attempting a head-on pass were turned away and Lieutenant Baker (77th Fighter Squadron) clobbered another Messerschmitt coming in from behind. The next day, after escorting the bombers back to the Dutch coast, the P-38s swooped on two airfields in the face of heavy flak; over Leck Lieutenant Everett was hit and quickly baled out.

Apart from 26 May, the Group would go out every day in May, ranging as far apart as St Quentin, France, Berlin and Sorau. Over Kiel (22 May) Major Gustke and Lieutenant Coon (77th Fighter Squadron) became separated and were bounced by seven Fw 190s who singled out the latter pilot. Gustke did knock down one Fw and finally maneuvered above and away from his adversaries; Coon was not so lucky and ended up a POW. Berlin (24 May) proved it was still a tough target, with thirty-three bombers being lost. The 20th Fighter Group succeeded in driving off those fighter attacks launched against the B-17s it was protecting. Among those flying this mission was Captain Jack Ilfrey a six kill veteran of the North African Campaign. He added to his tally by taking

Lieutenant "Lucky" Lowman (left) flew Sergeant Ed Beck to Northern Ireland in BOND BABY, the Groups two seat P-51B. Beck got the trip by winning a war bond drive prize. The "war weary" P-51B had two Malcolm hoods and the second seat was installed in the area formerly used for radio equipment. The tail bar X code had a small W on either side of the X to indicate the aircraft was in the "war weary" class.

down two Bf 109s. "Taking down" could literally be applied to his second victim; a head-on clash resulted in the Messerschmitt striking Jack's right wing-tip which threw it into a spin before it tumbled down in flames. Ilfrey controlled his own spin and limped back to base to arrive well after anybody else, the wing-tip bent and shredded. This feisty warrior would go on to command the 79th Fighter Squadron and evade capture after being shot down in France on 13 June. Not so fortunate was his fellow 79th Fighter Squadron pilot, Lieutenant Huarte, who was last seen near Hamburg trailing on one engine; he ended up a POW in Stalag Luft III.

The sole short-range mission flown until the month-end was to Brussels, but it cost the Group all its remaining casualties of the month. Strafing targets of opportunity, first Lieutenant Boele (55th Fighter Squadron) had one engine set on fire and fatally crashed. Two 79th Fighter Squadron pilots were also brought down, Lieutenant Bench being killed and Lieutenant Watson being captured. Strangely, Boele's body was never found. Flak was just the most obvious hazard on such low-level assaults, as Lieutenant Smelz discovered when he struck a high-tension line which disabled one engine but thankfully left his P-38 still airworthy. The 55th Fighter Squadron pilot's fortune was matched by Lieutenant Salzman (79th Fighter Squadron) who was severely wounded in one arm and the thigh by flak. With part of the control column shot away he prepared to bale out but realized he still had control of the P-38 and decided to head for home. His right engine seized as he crossed the English coast and he limped into the nearest available airfield, collapsing in the cockpit just after stopping.

The mission on 31 May was a "double-header" with escort duties in the morning to Hamm/Osnabruck and a dive-bombing mission against a

A group armorer loads ammunition into the wing guns of a P-51D Mustang. The P-51D had six .50 caliber machine guns while the earlier P-51B had only four. The instruction on the bay cover cover bore sighting and loading of the weapons.

Lieutenant Hanzo of the 79th FIghter Squadron dressed in the standard flying coveralls with one leg pouch. His flying boots are Royal Air Force style. Lieutenant Hanzo was shot down and captured on 11 February 1944.)

heavily-laden airfield. This target was haze covered and the Group attacked Rheine instead. The great bonus accruing from supplementary strafing attacks within each mission was the destruction of no less than forty-one locomotives.

A pair of outbound P-51Ds of the 79th Fighter Squadron. Lieutenant Heiden flew MC-H, while Lieutenant Merriman flew MC-M, named *ALMY TOO*. Both are early P-51Ds without the fin fillet.

OKIE BLOKE IV, flown by Bill Smith of the 55th Fighter Squadron during the Summer of 1944, was the fourth aircraft to carry the name. (Via Larry Davis)

A group of 79th Fighter Squadron pilots ride out to their aircraft in one of the group's jeeps. Lieutenant Pogue (left) sets on the hood, while Lieutenant Beschen is seated in the rear.

THE BUTCHER BOY **was flown by Captain Ted Slanker of the 77th Fighter Squadron. The aircraft name came from an incident in flight school, when Ted "buzzed" a herd of cattle, causing them to stampede. When all had settled down, several of the cattle were dead and the name stuck.**

D-DAY TO FRANTIC VI

June 1944 - a month of tremendous import for the Allied quest for Victory involved the 20th Fighter Group in the largest number of missions (thirty-five) it would complete in any one month. Most would be tied in with D-Day and the first vital steps in enlarging the Normandy bridge head to prevent any chances of a second and even more disastrous Dunkirk.

The first two sorties were standard bomber escorts around Paris and the Pas de Calais. Clear indications that something "Big" was looming came on 5 June when the Group senior staff returned from a conference with General Anderson bearing a multitude of charts, maps and associated documents. Sure enough, an early evening briefing confirmed that a mighty armada of vessels was about to depart their Southern English ports carrying Allied forces to Normandy. The Group instituted patrols over the convoys between approximately 1700 and 2130, these being flown first by the 77th Fighter Squadron and 79th Fighter Squadron until relieved by the 55th Fighter Squadron.

History has recorded that the anticipated counter-thrusts to Operation OVERLORD never materialized, so thoroughly duped was the enemy by the Allies pre-Invasion strategy. The lack of aerial opposition was an anti-climax to the Allied airmen in particular, keyed up to expect the Luftwaffe to intervene en masse.

A pair of P-51D Mustangs of the 77th Fighter Squadron parked on the grass at Glatton, the home base of the 457th Bomb Group during the Spring of 1945. The aircraft in the foreground has the upper wing and elevator surfaces camouflaged as well as the fin leading edge. LC-Xbar was flown by Lieutenant Kerns and LC-B was PAPER DOLL, flown by Captain Herbert. Lieutenant Kern has had the White in the fuselage national insignia "grayed" out.

LI'L DADDY was assigned to Lieutenant Bill Martin of the 55th Fighter Squadron. The aircraft in the background is an early production P-51D without the fin fillet. Both aircraft carry the early Black and White group nose markings. The Mustang carries a Spitfire type rear view mirror mounted on the upper canopy framing. This type of mirror was preferred by most pilots over the U.S. type.

This scattered pile of wreckage is all that remains of the P-51D Mustang flown by Lieutenant Woodrow Williams of the 79th FIghter Squadron. The aircraft was reportedly struck by lightning on 17 July 1944 and torn apart. Miraculously, Williams parachute deployed even though he was still strapped to his seat. Both pilot and seat landed safely with Williams receiving only minor injuries. Lieutenant WIlliams finished his combat tour in November of 1944.

This P-51D Mustang of the 55th Fighter Squadron mangled the starboard wing trailing edge and propeller in either a landing or take off accident. Prior to being transferred to the 55th Fighter Squadron, the Mustang had been assigned to Lieutenant Fiebelkorn of the 79th Fighter Squadron.

This 79th Fighter Squadron P-51D was named *GLENGARY GUY.* It had the upper fuselage, wings and elevators camouflaged in Olive Drab, with an outline of Natural Metal around the tail markings. The aircraft in the background is the group's UC-64 Norseman communications aircraft.

On D-Day, the invasion fleet was patrolled in relays with the 20th Fighter Group contributing by dispatching each squadron three times. The first took off at 0346 and the last at 2113 with each patrol lasting ninety minutes. Perhaps the only pilot not experiencing a sense of anti-climax was Major Weymss; he under-shot the airfield in the darkness and poor visibility existing as the 77th Fighter Squadron landed off the last patrol around 2300, but stepped out of his wrecked P-38 with minor injuries.

These patrols (apart from 9 June, when bad weather intervened) were the order of the day up to 10 June. The monotony was broken this day when the fifth patrol led by Colonel Rau disengaged and turned inland to Granville where trucks and other transport were worked over, with Cy Wilson destroying eight ammunition trucks.

On 12 June the bombers ranged after tactical targets inland and the 20th Fighter Group went out as a complete Group to catch any enemy aircraft over Brest. This yielded no results, so the Group descended for strafing - at a cost. Lieutenant Gese (77th Fighter Squadron) baled out from his crippled fighter and landing intact. He managed to contact Resistance sources and later return to England. Lieutenant Jacobson (77th Fighter Squadron) was last seen as the Group reformed but never came home. Meanwhile, Captain McLary (55th Fighter Squadron) was back at Kingscliffe recovering from a take-off crash. One engine - and soon after the P-38 - caught fire and a hasty belly-landing was effected several miles from the base.

A second mission this day was a Droop-snoot attack on Loire River bridges. Finding the Primary clouded-over, a rail and a road bridge at Amboise were struck, with hits at one end of the latter structure. Lieutenant Fiebelkorn was forced by fuel shortage to land on a Normandy beach-head Landing Strip where he discovered his 1,000 pound bomb was still in place. Lieutenants Kendrick and Kuemmerle (77th Fighter Squadron) ran into flak near Caen. The latter managed to gain Allied lines before crash-landing, but Kendrick was not so lucky. As he zoomed upwards, his left wing engine and fuel tank burst into flames. His attempt to get out of the doomed P-38 was badly compromised when only the right-side canopy panel partially released. Being occupied with maintaining direction and pitch control he could release the left-hand panel, an operation which required both hands. Straining to push himself through the small right-side gap while standing on the cockpit seat had no initial effect as the fighter now snapped into a spin. Miraculously, as it snapped into its third turn Kendrick was squeezed out to tumble between the tail booms. Pulling his rip-cord he was soon brought up with a breath-taking jerk and floated down to a stand-up landing, probably due to his dinghy pack acting as a spring as he fell down on his rear.

Kendrick knew he had been sighted by the Germans so he made haste to clear the area. He passed near his P-38 which had impacted at a flat angle and, although mangled, was still identifiable. A deep ditch between two grain fields provided cover but even so he had to proceed on all-fours, an action which rapidly tired him out. The ditch petered out and Kendrick decided to rest under some bushes which hopefully would conceal him from his pursuers.

A young Frenchman came up and Kendrick spoke the one word

Captain John Tennant shrugs resignedly mext to the mangled rear fuselage of KI-W. The damage was caused by another Mustang in a taxi accident. Tennent served from 15 May to 9 December 1944, scoring a total of three kills and logging a total of 270 combat hours.

Lieutenant Colonel Russell Gustke (middle) receives a "farewell" gift on completion of his third combat tour in April of 1945. He made one tour in North Africa, and two at Kingscliffe. Major Nicholls (77th Fighter Squadron Commander) does the honors while Colonel Montomery (20th Fighter Group Commander) looks on.

"American" which elicited an unintelligible response. He moved on but was almost immediately spotted by a young boy who glanced at him and went away. Any hopes that either might assist him later were dashed by the appearance of a Wehrmacht officer who all too easily picked Kendrick out from his inadequate hiding place and arrested him. The steady drain in pilots continued next day when a glide and dive-bombing attack was made on a rail bridge at La Possiniere and a road bridge at Montjean. Solid strikes were recorded on the former while a complete span was deleted on the latter. Two pilots were lost in subsequent strafing attacks. Lieutenant Quinn (77th Fighter Squadron) was last seen going in on some trucks and became the latest KIA statistic. Captain Ilfrey (79th Fighter Squadron) was downed near Angers but his fate was much happier. While re-assembling after bombing Ilfrey spotted a railroad train in Lelion station. As his fire smashed into the locomotive, flak got his range and set his right engine afire. The smoke that filled the cockpit and choked him was whipped away as he released the canopy and baled out from a perilously low height, so low that his parachute was seen by Lieutenant Carpenter to oscillate once before he

Sergeant Hoppy Hopkins poses next to the rear fuselage of Captain Ilfrey's P-51D, *Happy Jacks Go Buggy*.

Eleanor Rogers (right) and Ina Bacon standing in a Red Cross marked weapons carrier. They were two of the Red Cross personnel assigned to Kingscliffe.

thumped into the wall of a farmhouse (after the war Carpenter told Ilfrey that his immediate thought was "Too dammed close, Jack", probably thinking that the impact had been lethal). Lieutenant Heiden considered landing to pick the downed pilot up but was put off by the poor terrain.

Discarding his flying gear he became aware of a man with a pitchfork from whom he asked which direction was North. Apart from his determination to regain Allied lines, there was the desire not to be captured by those whom he had just been strafing. Their reaction might prove extremely rough, not to say fatal.

The funeral pyre of his P-38 with its ammunition exploding was visible as he struck out through hedges and across fields until exhausted. A pause to rest, then he headed off at a steadier pace along a country road. He was only a few minutes further on when two boys on bicycles came up behind. To their inquiries he confirmed that he was indeed the "American Aviator" from the crashed aircraft. Accompanying them to the village of Andigne, Ilfrey was hidden in the living quarters of the cafe belonging to one of the boys' family. For the next few days he helped in menial tasks such as wood-chopping and floor sweeping. The latter duty in the cafe provided him with his first "scare" when some German soldiers walked in; he beat a steady but very nervous retreat

***LIL SIS* of the 77th Fighter Squadron warms up its engine before the start of another mission. The nose art extends over the group markings on the nose and both aircraft have colored rudders.**

Two rows of P-51Ds with *Chatanooga Choo Choo* of the 79th Fighter Squadron in the foreground. Behind her are Mustangs of the 77th Fighter Squadron and the line at the right are 55th Fighter Squadron aircraft.

back into the kitchen while wielding his broom.

His continued presence was becoming known to a worrying number of the villagers. This fact, along with indications over the family's clandestine radio that the Allied advance was bogged down, made Ilfrey decide that he must abandon his original intention of staying put until the region was liberated and head out again. He persuaded the daughter of the family into parting with her precious bicycle; in the meantime an Identity Card in the name of "Jacques Robert" was obtained with its history relating to a farmer who had been injured and rendered deaf in a bombing raid on Angers.

A six day trek lay ahead of him with several sticky situations. Towards the end of the first day he inadvertently followed the road which cut through a Luftwaffe airfield. Unable to turn back from the sentry-box without arousing suspicion he played out his "deaf" act to the sentry with no success. Fortunately his condition was accepted by the Hauptmann whom the sentry called to sort out the situation. As he traversed the airfield he pondered upon whether he could hi-jack one of several Bf 109s on the field, having flown a captured example while serving in North Africa, but quickly dismissed the idea as too dangerous. An unpleasant sight on the field was the wrecks of two P-38s.

The problem of a punctured tire the next morning was resolved by a passing priest who took him to his monastery where he stayed overnight, being fed and watered. Day four involved a further two scary incidents. First, the German truck convoy he had been cycling with for some time came under attack by a P-38 flight; he sped for a nearby slope from where he witnessed the annihilation of all six vehicles. Later on,

A group of 55th Fighter Squadron ground crewmen, including Ed Beck (left) are dwarfed by an RAF Stirling bomber at Wittering. The bomber was a Stirling Mk I which had been retired from active service and was being used by a Heavy Conversion Unit (HCU) training future bomber crews.

RAF aircraft shared facilities with the 20th. Two extremes of British wartime design are parked on the grass, the huge Lancaster bomber and a Tiger Moth biplane trainer. The Lancaster was the RAF's primary bomber and the Tiger Moth was the primary training aircraft for the RAF. A number of Tiger Moths were also used by 8th Air Force units as communications aircraft.

he was accosted by a lone German soldier who demanded the bicycle. Ilfrey's protests that he needed his transport looked like being of no avail when salvation arrived in the form of a Wehrmacht truck which obviously provided the soldier with a surer form of travel. Luck indeed!

As he approached Flers he witnessed the bombing by B-17s of its railyard, but noted as he then passed through the town that many surrounding houses had shared the yard's fate. The next day he had problems crossing the river at Conde where all bridges had been destroyed by bombing; fortunately the broken remnants of one structure permitted him to pick him way cautiously over the river. Arriving in Eurecy he found it packed full of soldiers in full battle gear. This, along with the sound of Allied gunfire confirmed he was very close to the battle line. Contact with yet another French family, who sheltered him over night revealed that the wife had lived for several years in Baltimore. The next day he surrendered his bicycle to two soldiers supporting their wounded comrade. Now on foot he headed west through Fontenay, also packed with soldiers. Two miles further he went to cross a clearing only to be shouted at by some personnel entrenched to one side. Crawling over to them he continued to play his deaf act. Then, when one of the soldiers was wounded by fragments from a shell burst, he was ordered to take the man in a wheel-barrow to the nearest Casualty Station, a long-winded and tiresome chore. As he turned to leave the Station one of the Medics shouted "Hey." Thinking his disguise had been penetrated he faced the man, only to be handed a cigarette and a chocolate bar as

Gun camera footage from fighters of the 20th Fighter Group. A locomotive (below) is shot up during a very low level attack. The scenes at right were repeated some 211 times during the 20th's tour of duty in the Second World War. Both of the aircraft streaming smoke after being hit are Luftwaffe Bf 109s.

Janey Girl II From Texas goes to full power on the Pierced Steel Planking (PSP) parking area as it prepares to taxi out to the runway. The spinner tip of this 79th Fighter Squadron Mustang was left in Natural Metal.

thanks for his humanitarian action!

Free from scrutiny again, Ilfrey met two boys who indicated the position of Allied forces. Not long after, he ran across an intersection of hedgerows and behind them were a number of British soldiers who challenged the ragged "Frenchman." His attempts to explain his circumstances were greeted with natural suspicion, and it was not until he reached the British Headquarters that he was accepted. This was due in no small measure to a U. S. Liaison Officer's presence; not only could he question Ilfrey about his "American background", but he also hailed from the pilot's home state of Texas. A quick return to England and further questioning was followed by Ilfrey resuming his combat career at Kingscliffe (normally evaders were not encouraged to resume combat in the same Operational Theater but this rule in Ilfrey's case was either ignored or "evaded.")

The four days following the 13 June proved very expensive with seven pilots MIA. Ground attacks around Central/Northern Holland (l4 June) resulted in Captain Williams (77th Fighter Squadron) and Lieutenant Spencer (55th Fighter Squadron) being downed by train based flak; the former baled out but Spencer crashed on the other side of the train he was attacking. Over France the next day, Lieutenant Perra (77th Fighter Squadron) was taken down. He was reported by a French eye-witnesses at Les Corvees to be low down when one engine was disabled by flak.

Originally deigned as a dive bomber, the Vultee A-35 Vengence was assigned as target tows, and general "hack" aircraft by a number of groups, including the 20th. This A-35 was assigned to Kingscliffe sometime during 1944/45. The RAF and Royal Australian Air Force made good use of the Vengence in its original role of dive bombing in the Far East.

The Black and White checkered vehicle was the 20th Fighter Group;s Mobile Flying Control Vehicle, used to control ground movements on the field and traffic within the airfield boundary.

The P--38 went into a spin and although Perra jumped he was too close to the ground to be saved by his chute. Having stripped his body of all identification the Germans refused permission for his burial in the town cemetery and he was interred in the field where he fell. The mayor noted the aircraft serial (2194067) and name (LITTLE BUG) at the time, and these details were provided to the l0th Service Group personnel who took part in the 1944 Armistice Day ceremony. It was, however, some time later before the anonymous flier was identified as Walter Perra. On the same mission Colonel Rau was fortunate to survive flak hits on his stabilizer; only his strength enabled him to pull the P-38 out of its resultant nose-down attitude.

Not only was the 16 June mission scrubbed but Major Lobinger went in near Boreham and his aircraft exploded. Glide-bombing a bridge at Corbie (17 June) not only brought no results, but increased the Group's gloom with a trio of losses. Two pilots, Lieutenant Hairston (77th Fighter Squadron) and Lieutenant Ryan (79th Fighter Squadron), baled out but the latter's chute tragically did not open. Lieutenant Earl Smith (79th Fighter Squadron) was the third loss, but unlike Hairston he would evade capture, being one of ten group personnel to avoid becoming a POW. Apart from Lieutenant Peterson (79th Fighter Squadron) suffering engine failure and crash-landing near Kingscliffe (19 June) nothing of significance occurred until 22 June, when another flak victim, Lieutenant Pearson (55th Fighter Squadron) was seen to explode.

The run of misfortune was marginally eased on 25 June when the second of two missions over France led to an encounter with around fifteen Bf 109s. These dived away when called in but Colonel Wilson, leading the chase in a P-38 equipped with aileron boost and dive-flaps, steadily over-hauled one and nailed him. Wilson's windshield, however, cracked in the process.

The use of drop-tanks as auxiliary bombs was now a regular feature of most missions. On 27 June, a troop train was among the targets. Lieutenant Moncrieff (77th Fighter Squadron) went so low he scraped through the tree tops and on return to base had to land without his nose gear. Feeling the main landing gear beginning to fold on touch-down Lieutenant Colonel Johnson (Deputy Group Commander) pulled up and

After he survived the destruction of his Mustang when it was hit by lightning on 27 July 1944, Lieutenant Woodrow Williams of the 79th Fighter Squadron became known throughout the group as the "luckiest pilot int he 20th Fighter Group."

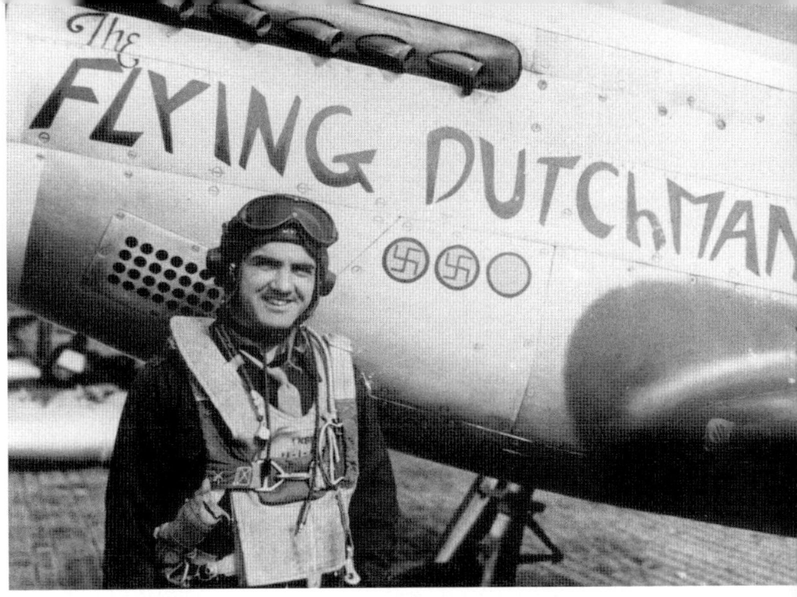

Captain Earl "Pappy" Hower of the 55th Fighter Squadron poses by the nose of his P-51D named *FLYING DUTCHMAN* (KI-N). Two of the circles on the nose contain kill markings. Hower was assigned to the group in August of 1943 and completed his tour in September of 1944.

This going away party was for Major Jack Ilfrey (fifth from left), commander of the 79th Fighter Squadron (27 September to 9 December 1944). To his right was Major Wemyss (Group Operations Officer) while Colonel Montgomery (Group Commander) is on Jack's left. Major Gatterdam (55th Fighter Squadron commander) squats in the middle with Flight Lieutenant Nott (RAF Liaison Officer) along side of him (right).

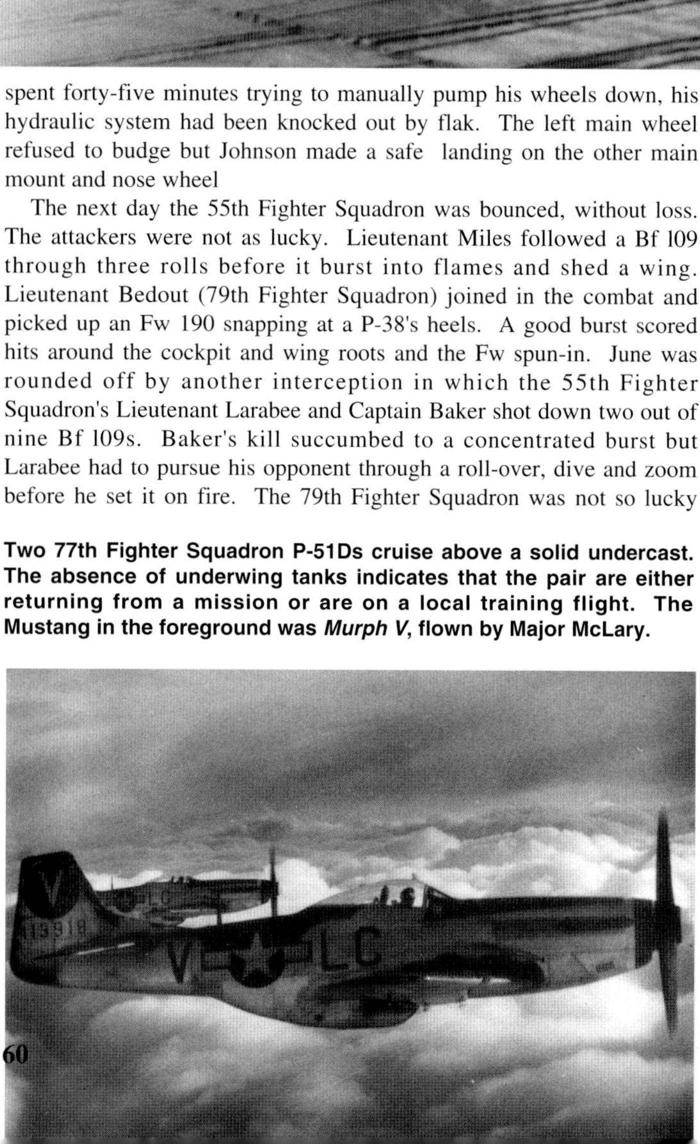

Lieutenant Schons of the 79th Fighter Squadron poses with two of his ground crew on the wing of the *"the VIRGIN'* during the Winter of 1944/45. The lack of underwing tanks indicates that the Lieutenant is either going or has just returned on a local flight

spent forty-five minutes trying to manually pump his wheels down, his hydraulic system had been knocked out by flak. The left main wheel refused to budge but Johnson made a safe landing on the other main mount and nose wheel

The next day the 55th Fighter Squadron was bounced, without loss. The attackers were not as lucky. Lieutenant Miles followed a Bf 109 through three rolls before it burst into flames and shed a wing. Lieutenant Bedout (79th Fighter Squadron) joined in the combat and picked up an Fw 190 snapping at a P-38's heels. A good burst scored hits around the cockpit and wing roots and the Fw spun-in. June was rounded off by another interception in which the 55th Fighter Squadron's Lieutenant Larabee and Captain Baker shot down two out of nine Bf 109s. Baker's kill succumbed to a concentrated burst but Larabee had to pursue his opponent through a roll-over, dive and zoom before he set it on fire. The 79th Fighter Squadron was not so lucky when ordered down on fifteen Bf 109s; not only did the enemy evade in clouds but three P-38s were hit by flak as they climbed back up.

In mid-June two pilots turned up who everyone though were lost. Colonel Bob Montgomery and Lieutenant Harry Bisher. Shot down in Northern France and Belgium respectively, each had been taken in by the Resistance and channeled as far as Paris, where they were reunited. Bob had arrived here ahead of Harry and was accompanied by a Canadian and a P-47 pilot. The latter had got his revenge on "Authority" (in the shape of Bob) while concealed at a previous location. A snap German raid forced the trio onto the roof with Bob laying just below his fellow-American who now announced his bladder was full. Despite Bob's threat as to what he would inflict on his desperate colleague should he not "hold it", it took the Germans such a long time to conclude their search that the inevitable happened.

While passing through Limoges rail station in a strung-out formation (thus allowing the others to evade should one in the party be apprehended) Harry had the un-nerving experience of being approached by a woman who tried to engage him in conversation. Thankfully his muttering "I don't know" in his very limited French, seemed to do the trick, because the woman desisted and turned away. His particular problems continued in Toulouse when, with each evader split up and assigned a guide, Harry's led him around a succession of locations - and finally right into a German patrol. Fortunately they were able to out-run the soldiers.

Linked up again, the Kingscliffe duo set off for the Pyrenees. Climbing these mountain heights was dreadful for Bob who had suffered burns and a heavy landing. Deserted by their "guides" with false promises that the Spanish border was just over the next ridge, they stag-

Two 77th Fighter Squadron P-51Ds cruise above a solid undercast. The absence of underwing tanks indicates that the pair are either returning from a mission or are on a local training flight. The Mustang in the foreground was *Murph V*, flown by Major McLary.

Captain John Taylor of the 79th Fighter Squadron was forced to make a wheels up landing when he experienced problems just after take off on 26 February 1945. A mangled propeller and a heavily damaged underside are testimony to the heavy impact. The aircraft was a total "write-off."

gered on for a full three days before achieving their goal.

July continued the mix of strategic and tactical targets for the bombers as they strove to both support the Allied armies in their advance, while also keeping pressure on the enemy's ability to produce the means to sustain the Wehrmacht and Luftwaffe's resistance.

The first completed month's mission (4 July) was a double-header with escort duty followed by a strafing brief which netted, among other results, thirty-six locomotives. Ten P-38s were damaged on this run and Lieutenant Riddle (79th Fighter Squadron) was killed in a crash on returning to England. Seven more locomotives the next day added to the group's "locobusting" reputation. An unlucky He 177 was also dispatched by Lieutenant Colonel Johnson.

The chance to indulge in fighter-to-fighter combat was steadily receding by mid-1944, the main strength of the Luftwaffe having been savaged in the great air battles of March and April. It was now a question of being in the right location to intercept the groups of Fw 190s and Bf 109s sent up to hopefully engage any section of the bomber-stream without fighter cover. These STURMGRUPPEN would usually come in on the unfortunate bombers from behind and try to demolish as many as possible, before escorting fighters could be summoned to assist the beleaguered crews.

On 7 July, the Group probably engaged such a force as they covered B-24s into Halle. An estimated fifty Me 410s and 100 Fw190s and Bf 109s were picked up, some of which actually bounced the 55th Fighter Squadron. In turn, the 77th Fighter Squadron attacked another element of the enemy force. For the 55th Fighter Squadron, Lieutenants Loehnart and Hallberg raised the unit's score by two and one Bf 109s respectively. Four fell to the 77th Fighter Squadron, being an Me 410 apiece for Captain Morris and Lieutenant Adams and an Fw 190 apiece for Lieutenants Fernandes and Clark. The sole Group loss was an expensive one however; Captain Morris was caught in the return fire from the barrette-guns mounted on the Me 410's rear fuselage and he went down to become a POW. "Slick" Morris had been with the Group since August of 1942 and was one of the first Aces along with Captain Graham.

The strafing brief on the August covered rail and road traffic south of Paris. This mission raked in another tally of successes. Fuel tanks were dropped on Giens marshaling yards and on a tree-shrouded freight-train close by, huge fires being started. Even more spectacular was the detonation of what was most likely an ammunition train by the 79th Fighter Squadron. Lieutenant Carpenter added to the record by closing on a massive Ju 290 transport and downing it in flames.

One of the most critical stages of a mission was take-off in what were heavily (and often over-laden) aircraft. On 12 July, Lieutenant Robbins (79th Fighter Squadron) cracked open the throttles but soon found himself lagging behind his Flight Leader. Adding more power only sufficed to lift the P-38 off the runway, at which point it sagged inexorably

***TRUDY* was assigned to the 77th Fighter Squadron. The mechanic posing with the Mustang was Sergeant Schill, who was killed when he ran his bicycle into a moving propeller.**

This 79th Fighter Squadron P-51D, flown by Flight Officer Halloran, ground looped on 12 June 1945. The starboard landing gear failed and the crash caused heavy damage to the starboard wing. This Mustang was previously flown by Lieutenant Jones and was named *Nina Merle III/Nancy.*

A formation of 77th Fighter Squadron Mustangs cruises above a solid undercast. The aircraft are carrying 108 gallon pressed paper drop tanks.

downwards. Attempts to jettison the drop-tanks barely succeeded before the aircraft touched ground and scraped along -- straight for the bomb-dump. Fire quickly enveloped the fuselage and Robbins desperately bashed his head and shoulders against the jammed top canopy. Even when this was opened he still had problems since his helmet lead to the radio outlet would not release. Frantically pulling the helmet off he stumbled away from the aircraft, his uniform, gloves and hair on fire, to collapse a few feet away. Here he was smothered in blankets by the crash crew, who also started to extinguish the fire. Transferred to the 49th Station Hospital, the badly burnt pilot now faced a series of operations to rebuild his face and hands, procedures which lasted three years. The gallantry of the crash crew in saving Robbins and fighting the fire which threatened the bomb dump was recognized, with three of the men being awarded the Soldiers Medal.

That day also Lieutenant Ruie (55th Fighter Squadron) confirmed the inherent strength of the P-38 airframe when he crashed off a non-operational flight. His aircraft scythed through the tops of some very sturdy trees but, although totally wrecked, the P-38 delivered its pilot to earth completely uninjured. The next day Lieutenant Dungan baled out over the Thames Estuary when both engines failed, to be quickly picked up by a small boat.

Bastille Day (14 July) was celebrated over France, the Group using bombs and drop-tanks to wreak havoc on road and rail links West of Paris. A marshaling yard, a rail tunnel mouth and an ammunition train felt their power. The tunnel roof and sides collapsed while the train's destruction was achieved by just one pilot, Lieutenant Anderson. This overall contribution by the 55th Fighter Squadron was added to in the air, when Lieutenant Mullins shot down an Bf 109 which used up most of his ammunition. The 79th Fighter Squadron mangled another yard and two trains, one of which blew apart. Lieutenants Fiebelkorn and Arthaud (77th Fighter Squadron) horned in on five Fw 190s near Rheims and shared in the destruction of one. Only Lieutenant Hunt (55th Fighter Squadron) was MIA having baled out near Menehould but would in time return safely. Major Low with one engine “out” over-shot on landing at Sibson close to Kingscliffe. His aircraft turned over, but the Major was dug out with minor injuries.

Returning from Saarbrucken next day, Lieutenant Klink lost his second engine close to the English coast and became the latest Group member to sample the “hospital-ity” of the ASR Service. More strafing of French road and rail links was succeeded by three escort runs to Peenemunde, Kempton and Leipzig. On the Kempton mission Lieutenant Hillyard (79th Fighter Squadron) was on fire over the Dutch coast when he indicated he was jumping. He was not seen to vacate the P-38 as it plunged into the sea and still is listed as MIA.

A major change was instituted on the Leipzig mission, the change from P-38s to P-51s. The normal practice of switching aircraft types as a whole Group was discarded in favor of each Squadron converting in turn. In this manner, the Group could carry out missions instead of having to step down from operations until the switch was fully completed. The 55th Fighter Squadron flew their new charges as the “B” Group, while the other squadrons formed the “A” Group. The Mannheim mission on 21 July was the 77th Fighter Squadron’s first P-51 mission and

Colonel Bob Montgomery was assigned to the 20th Fighter Group in August of 1940. He was promoted to Group Executive Officer in November of 1943, and was shot down in February of 1944. He evaded capture and returned to the unit in June. He was assigned as Deputy Group Commander in November of 1944 and became Group Commander in December.

These two P-51Bs of the 55th Fighter Squadron carry the same individual aircraft letter, Q. The aircraft in the foreground, Q-bar, still has the original P-51B canopy, while the aircraft in the background appears to have a “Malcomb” canopy. The Black spinner indicates that these Mustangs have been assigned to Operation Training status.

Lieutenant Jurgens of the 79th Fighter Squadron confers with another squadron officer in the cockpit of his Mustang. There are six kill markings on the canopy frame and two on the fuselage below the canopy, suggesting different tallys for different pilots.

the Group was completely re-equipped for the Brest mission on 24 July.

No enemy aircraft were engaged during the transitional period and what combat there was before the month-end involved individual pilots. On 29 July Lieutenants Moncrieff and Adams (77th Fighter Squadron) were aborting with engine problems when they crossed the rear of a formation of Bf l09s. Notwithstanding the odds (50 to 2) they circled to close in from behind and in quick succession shot down one and two fighters respectively. Seeing another large formation approaching, discretion over-came valor and they high-tailed it for home. Bad weather over Kingscliffe forced many pilots to land away at airfields in East Anglia.

If Lieutenant Dempsey (77th Fighter Squadron) had any doubt about the value of aircraft recognition as a pertinent subject it was dispelled on 31 July. Separated from his flight he picked up eight " P-51s" which, as he closed in, materialized into Bf 109s. His resultant disengagement and pursuit by his "friends" ended quickly and to his advantage as he pulled up into the overcast!

The elements could be as lethal as any human opponent and this was vividly demonstrated on 27 July by Lieutenant Williams (79th Fighter Squadron). Heading out, his P-51 simply exploded (most probably due to a lightning strike). Few pilots survived such an incident, but Williams recovered consciousness on the ground, still strapped to his seat. Not only did he survive the blast but somehow his chute had opened and supported the weight of man and equipment to a sound landing. Following hospitalization he completed his tour and returned home in November.

August opened with two notable events. The Group escorted 3rd Bomb Division B-17s who dropped arms to the Resistance deep in France. Finishing up with this mission, was Lieutenant Colonel Herbert Johnson (Deputy Group Commander) who, in over 300 operational

Lieutenant Tom Gardner of the 79th Fighter Squadron poses with his ground crew, Sergeant May and Staff Sergeant Spjut around the cockpit of Georgia Boy during the Winter of 1944/45. The building in the background houses the squadron armament section.

Lieutenant Dick Iehle's 55th Fighter Squadron P-51D Mustang also carried two names. *Green Eyes* was on the right canopy rail and *Ginny* was carried on the left canopy rail. The fuselage national marking was "Grayed" out to make it less noticeable.

A pair of 79th Fighter Squadron P-51Ds had a taxi acciednt resulting in a bent propeller for *PEGGY JO*. *PEGGY* has a checkerboard above the group marking on the nose. The Mustang in the background ha s a gap between the group marking and the anti-glare panel on the nose.

hours, had chalked up five kills, including the Group's first ever. A record number of sixty-three P-51s were dispatched; since transitioning from the P-38 the abort rate had been virtually nil.

Lieutenant Nelson (55th Fighter Squadron) became the latest loss when he failed to survive a crash near Peterborough on 2 August. Escorts to Saarbrucken and Peenemunde with strafing thrown in occupied the next two days. In the latter instance an airfield west of the research establishment was selected for "the treatment" along with some E and R-Boats moored close by on the Baltic waters. As Lieutenant Don Reihmer (77th Fighter Squadron CO) skimmed across the airfield he was hit in the engine but used his P-51's momentum to keep going a few miles out over the Baltic, at which point he abandoned the stricken fighter. He was soon immersed in the sea, but his difficulties were not over; he had extreme problems in releasing his chute harness due to the chest straps immobilizing his arms and preventing him turning the harness release. Somehow he released his aim and inflated his Mae West before clambering into his dinghy. He removed his trousers in order to dry out the seat, which turned out to be a mistake because, when he put them on again all the water he had laboriously scooped out of the dinghy slopping back in as the dinghy side was pushed under by his physical exertions.

The sea was cold even in late Summer and during the ensuing night he hailed a German light-ship but was not heard. Next morning his condition was such that he abandoned his original intention of heading for Denmark and tried to steer south without much success. The prospect of dying from exposure was unpleasant but had to be faced as nightfall again fell. Fortunately there was a full moon and this would be a strong factor in Reihmer's salvation. During the night he awoke from doze to see a ship bearing down on him. Its wash swept him mercifully to the side and his cries for help were answered by the crew, who stopped the vessel and launched a lifeboat, which nearly sank due to the fact that the drain plug had been removed in Lubeck and not reinserted! The SKARSBORG was Swedish and within a day or so he was landed in Sweden. A few weeks later he was flown back to Leuchars, Scotland aboard a B-24. (His bale-out had been witnessed by POWs at Barth, among them Royal Frey who recognized the P-51's markings as a 20th Fighter Group aircraft, and assumed Reihmer had probably perished).

In addition to Captain Reihmer's loss on the mission, Captain Baker, a 55th Fighter Squadron original pilot and Squadron Operations Officer was killed when he crashed on take-off.

A good run of aerial victories between 5 and 9 August commenced over Holland when the 77th Fighter Squadron and 79th Fighter Squadron were detached to oppose over sixty Bf 109s. Captain Gilbertson and Lieutenant Fiebelkorn (77th Fighter Squadron) and Lieutenant Binkley (79th Fighter Squadron) got one apiece while other pilots claimed one probable and three damaged. In turn, Lieutenant Fernandes (77th Fighter Squadron) was killed. The next day, near Berlin, the 55th Fighter Squadron came down on some enemy fighters, the result being an Fw 190 to Lieutenants Schmelz and Mansker and a Do 217 to Lieutenant Klink. The 79th Fighter Squadron scored too, including a Bf l09 which Lieutenant Rader "frightened" into diving into a lake without firing a shot. Lieutenant Alexander knocked down two. The 79th Fighter Squadron's Lieutenants Lewis and Cameron each polished off a Bf l09 and damaged a second. Group losses were Lieutenant Whiteside (77th Fighter Squadron) who was declared MIA.

As good as these score-rates were, they were eclipsed on 9 August. A sweep around Munich was interrupted by a call for support from a

Lieutenant Colonel Montgomery poses for a photo for his mechanic. The aircraft name, *Gumpy*, intrudes into the group markings on the nose.

bomber formation. Some thirty Bf 109s were engaged by the 79th Fighter Squadron's Red Flight and White Flight challenged fifteen Fw 190s who were hitting the bombers. Finally, the 55th Fighter Squadron took on more Fw 190s. When the battle was over sixteen aircraft were missing from the Luftwaffe's inventory. Fourteen went to the 79th Fighter Squadron including two each to Captains Smith and Meyer, Lieutenant Bedout and Lieutenant Klatt (who also shared a third with Lieutenant Richard). Two squadrons totaling just over thirty P-51s had bested over 100 enemy fighters, proof indeed of the superior equipment and pilot skill of the 8th Fighter Command.

It was another week before more 'kills' were registered. During this time Lieutenant Lee Anderson (55th Fighter Squadron) and Lieutenant Rollins (77th Fighter Squadron) were lost (19 August), both were reported as baling out but neither actually survived. On 12 August, another pair were downed, Lieutenants Denbo (79th Fighter Squadron) and Lieutenant Clark (77th Fighter Squadron). Denbo's P-51 had been damaged by flak and he subsequently crashed over France on the way home. Clark's P-51 was struck by fragments of the train he was strafing and his engine lost power. He was about to crash-land when the engine started to pull again, so he pulled up to head for home. Two fellow-pilots now advised him he was losing fluid (probably engine coolant) and sure enough, a short time later the engine ceased running; Clark promptly jettisoned the canopy and jumped.

On touching down he noticed Lieutenants Hendricks and Robb circling and he thought they might attempt a landing to pick him up, but he waved them off as this seemed a risky venture. After they departed, Clark was approached by farmers laboring in the field where he had landed who took him to a place of concealment. Expecting to be channeled through Resistance hands for return to England, he was probably surprised to discover that the two men sent to escort him were FFI (French Forces of the Interior) who took him to a drop zone to await the arrival of an officer sent in to organize the FFI unit in that region. From here he was taken to a house near Sains-Richaumont where he would pass the next few weeks observing the German 7th Army in full retreat. The day finally arrived when the Germans were replaced by the U.S. 1st Army. Three soldiers turned up in a jeep inquiring after the "American pilot." It was forty-five days since Clark had been declared MIA back at Kingscliffe.

Going in towards Leipzig (16 August) with the 55th Fighter Squadron ahead, the 79th Fighter Squadron below, and the 77th Fighter Squadron to the left of the bombers , some fifty enemy fighters appeared and attacked. The 77th Fighter Squadron, with Colonel Wilson leading, turned into them and in quick succession the Colonel blasted an Fw 190

This Mustang of the 79th Fighter Squaron over-ran the runway and ended up in a soft field on 17 November 1944. The landing gear was ripped off and the aircraft was scrapped three days later. The aircraft was flown by Lieutenant Bradford.

While strafing Eperstedt Airfield on 9 February 1945, a Fw 190 fighter blew up in front of Major Merle J. Gilbertson's Mustang. The blast shattered his canopy but luckily only caused the Major some minor injuries. Even with his broken canopy, the 77th Fighter Squadron pilot went on to destroy another three enemy aircraft. The squadron destroyed a total of thirty-six on this mission, thirty-four on the ground and two in the air.

and a Bf 109 , both pilots baling out. Captains Gilbertson and McKeon scored further kills, as did the former's wingman, Lieutenant Rowlett; in his case he saved his leader from a Bf 109 that had closed on his tail. Two more squadron pilots (Lieutenants Arthaud and Adams) each shot down Bf l09s. The eighth and final kill went to Lieutenant Campbell (79th Fighter Squadron).

A double-header to Kiel and Brux on 24 August involved a very tiring days flying. Otherwise the single incident of note occurred in the morning when Lieutenant Larabee circled a B-24 crew who baled out off Holland and fixed their position for the ASR Service. Peenemunde was the target the next day and it was aerially quiet but was livened up when the 55th Fighter Squadron attacked a flying-boat base. When the P-51s departed, having beat up this and an nearby airfield, they had added over thirty destroyed and twenty-one damaged to their squadron tally. Only Lieutenant Bain was MIA having been seen to climb into his dinghy, which was being approached by a vessel; he became a Luftwaffe "guest" at Barth, very close to where he was shot down.

So far the month's kill/loss ratio was in the Group's favor. This position was rather altered on 27 August when the pilots were over Esbjerg, Denmark. An airfield which had just been bombed was selected for strafing but the few minutes delay in circling prior to committing the Group to a strafing run probably gave the flak gunners an extra degree of warning. Colonel Wilson, in the lead with the 55th Fighter Squadron, was hit as he crossed the airfield as were Lieutenants Kent and Harry Anderson, but they pulled away with the others. Wilson reported his P-51 was damaged and requested it be given the "once over" for external indication of strikes. A short time later, he was forced to exit his mortally wounded fighter and, after landing in the sea, was seen to clamber into his dinghy. Lieutenant Kent also baled out at this time and was picked up from the water by a Danish fishing vessel, only to later end up in German hands. Lieutenant Anderson attempted to ditch but was still in his P-51 when it sank. Wilson's loss rocked the Group. He had arrived on 12 April and in quick succession had become the commander of the 55th Fighter Squadron and then Group Commander in just two months. The 20th Fighter Group was blessed with firm but fair-minded commanders and Wilson fitted this pattern perfectly.

Completing a quartet of losses was Lieutenant Ed Doering (77th Fighter Squadron). If Captain Reihmer's period at sea seemed long then Doering's experience must have seemed to last a life-time. His P-51's engine was so damaged that after twenty minutes it over-heated. By then the Group was well out over the North sea, but Doering had little option other than to bale out, burning his arm in the process. Inflating his dinghy he climbed aboard - and was promptly sick. Although in his own words, "cold, wet and scared," he still confidently awaited the arrival of search planes who would guide an ASR launch to him. In fact, Group pilots did comb the region the next day but sighted nothing. Hardly surprisng given the vast sea in which to pinpoint the minuscule rubber-boat. For a full five days Doering drifted aimlessly until two German ships crossed his path and hauled him aboard. Being near the limits of physical endurance, he probably could not have cared less who picked him up. An initial period in a Danish prison was followed by shipment south to Dulag Luft (Oberursel) for interrogation and ultimate delivery to Stalag Luft I. While at Dulag Luft he was surprised to run into Colonel Wilson, naturally not being aware until then that the Colonel had shared Ed's fate:

One of the primary missions during August was Loco-bashing, with

Captain Kies of the 79th FIghter Squadron was flying this Mustang named *LITTLE ROUE* (French for wheel) when he was badly wounded on a strafing attack . He made it back to Kingscliffe, but his combat career was at an end. The Mustang also carried the names *SISSY* and *SANDY* on the canopy frame.

This 77th Fighter Squadron P-51D had its rear fuselage neary torn off the aircraft and is only fit for scrap. The incident occurred on 21 March 1945, however, Group records give no details of the crash.

The smoking remains of a 77th Fighter Squadron Mustang along side the taxiway. The position of the wreck indicates that the aircraft was on its landing gear when it caught fire. Details of the incident are unknown.

the Group ravaging railroads between Bad Kreuznach and Saarbrucken. Twenty-five locomotives were demolished with Major Anderson and Lieutenant Armstrong (77th Fighter Squadron) getting eight between them. Another 77th Fighter Squadron pilot, Lieutenant Armstrong baled out and was captured.

One mission would dominate September; in addition the Group would participate in operation MARKET GARDEN , the daring but flawed plan to drive into the Ruhr through Southern Holland. The first four missions were quiet escort runs while Stuttgart on 10 September only involved the 79th Fighter Squadron in ground strafing action when five aircraft were destroyed and one damaged.

A very different mission faced the pilots next morning, as they learned at briefing that they would spend that evening in Russia. FRANTIC VI was the latest in a series of "shuttle-bombing" missions; a regular feature of such operations was the triangular route out from England, then from Russia to Italy before returning to England.

Some seventy-one P-51s were assigned to cover 3rd Bomb Division Groups bombing Chemnitz before heading East with the bombers to land, in their case, at Piryatin. All but one of the spare aircraft within the total figure were used with sixty-four aircraft taking off. No opposition was encountered but only sixty-one P-51s landed together at Piryatin. Lieutenant Tennant (55th Fighter Squadron) was hit over the battle-lines but happily came down on the Russian side. Lieutenant Mansker (also 55th Fighter Squadron) landed elsewhere to arrive the next day. Lieutenant Horst (79th Fighter Squadron) finally ran out of fuel after his landing attempts at an airfield were thwarted by a threatening Russian fighter; he turned up in a C-47 having force-landed his powerless P-51.

Rested up, and having been treated to some robust Russian "entertainment", the pilots took off on 13 September for a wearying if uneventful flight to Fogia, Italy, the bombers striking Miscolez, Hungary enroute. While in Italy, Colonel Rau, recently returned from States-side leave and in full command again, was able to visit his wife who was serving in the WAC in Naples. The flight back to England was made by fifty-nine aircraft but Lieutenant Kuemmerle had to land at an airfield in France with engine trouble. Of the six pilots that did not return, two were still in Russia and four were in Italy.

MARKET GARDEN commenced on 17 September, but the 20th Fighter Group having the vast bulk of its strength only just returned from Italy that same day, did not operate until the next day. Then the pilots acted as area cover for B-24s dropping supplies to the lightly-armed paratroop forces. The low-level nature of the mission rendered the American crews vulnerable to flak, whose locations were difficult to pick out so that the U.S. fighters could counter-attack. Two similar missions (20 and 23 September) were conducted with little result. The overall operation ended on 24 September, when 2,000 of the 10,000 men of the British 1st Airborne Division re-crossed the swollen Rhine waters, after a spirited but unsuccessful defense of the bridge at Arnhem, whose retention was crucial to the Allied plan's success.

A pair of 79th Fighter Squadron Mustangs skirt an area of solid cloud cover. The aircraft in the foreground is a P-51B with a Malcolm hood and fin fillet, the aircraft in the background is P-51D. Both aircraft have camouflaged upper wing and stabilizer surfaces.

Of the five remaining September missions only one (28 September) threw up any action. Two 77th Fighter Squadron flights picked out a large group of Fw 190s and Bf 109s below and to their right. The willingness of a clearly out-numbered bunch of pilots to take on the Luftwaffe was the best indication of how the balance of aerial power had altered since early 1944. Lieutenant Fiebelkorn (Blue Leader) added two more to his tally in the initial combat at altitude. As the battle moved downwards, he came across Kothen airfield where a Fw 190 and Bf 109 were in the pattern; both were knocked down. Also scoring two kills was Lieutenant Robertson, while Lieutenant Slanker got one in the air and destroyed a twin engined fighter at its dispersal.

Run-up to the Rhine

Sixteen missions were briefed for October of which, the fourth mis-

Armed Forces Day 1945 display featured a mix of aircraft. Two 96th Bomb Group B-17s are flanked by 55th and 79 Fighter Squadron P-51s, as well as a "war weary" P-47 which carries 79th FS codes. The group's A-20 and Norseman hack aircraft are in the background.

Colonel Rau's P-51D Mustang, *"Gentle Annie"*, shares the grass with the aircraft assigned to other group commanders while at a conference called by General Francis H Griswold, commander of the 8th FIghter Command.

Chatanooga Choo Choo prepares to taxi out for another mission in the closing days of the Second World War. The Mustang carries a total of seven kill markings on the canopy frame. (via Larry Davis)

Captain John Hollis of the 79th Fighter Squadron flew this P-51D Mustang. He was credited with a M2 262 jet fighter kill on 10 April 1945. (Via Larry Davis)

Lieutenant R. H. Black of the 79th Fighter Squadron flew this P-51D Mustang named *BLACK's BIRD* during the Spring of 1945. (via Larry Davis)

sion on 6 October was the most notable. After escorting the bombers to Politz, the Group dropped down to hit seaplane bases stretching between Rostock and Lubeck on the Baltic. Some forty aircraft, ranging from tri-motored Do 24s, twin engined He 115s, Do 18s to single-engined Arado 196s were destroyed with the 55th Fighter Squadron getting twenty, the 77th Fighter Squadron thirteen and 79th Fighter Squadron seven; a further fourteen were claimed as damaged. The next day a return to Politz yielded four ground kills at almost as high a cost. First Captain McKeon and Lieutenant Robert Brown collided at altitude; thankfully both cleared their P-51s to float down into German hands. Then Lieutenant Dungan (77th Fighter Squadron) was hit by flak over Peenemunde, but was able to retain control of his aircraft long enough to bale out close to neutral Sweden (he would ultimately return to England).

This same day eight aircraft from the 55th and 79th Fighter Squadrons went out to support a couple of RAF Wellingtons. One of these dropped first its boat and then a large dinghy to the two men found near Texel. A further eight airmen in their dinghies were discovered and supplies were dropped to aid them.

Cologne became the focus of bombing attention between 14 and 17 October, but there was still little reaction from the Luftwaffe involving the Group. Two days later, Captain Willis Taylor (55th Fighter Squadron) was forced, presumably due to mechanical difficulties, to bale out of his fighter to land on the German side of the battle-line. Enemy fighters remained conspicuous by their absence for the remaining five October missions, but another pilot, Lieutenant Kautz (79th Fighter Squadron) was similarly forced to abandon his P-51 over

Holland when it caught fire. He joined Captain Taylor in a POW camp.

Operations were inevitably becoming more restricted with the onset of Winter, although the pace did not manifestly drop until December; bad weather coincided with the beginning of the Battle of the Bulge, grounding the Allied Air Forces just when they were needed to stem the German advance.

A novel aerial threat was encountered on 1 November when a Me 262 jet fighter struck at the 77th Fighter Squadron's Yellow Flight and probably accounted for Lieutenant Allison, who was killed. Revenge was extracted by Lieutenant Flowers who closed with the Me 262 while in a broad turn and landed strikes on the jet, after which the pilot baled out.

Merseburg, the next day, cost the Eighth forty bombers, but the 20th Fighter Group almost equaled this figure as a counter-blow. As the final Combat Bomb Wing aircraft was unloading its bomb load, enemy fighters descended on the formation. Colonel Montgomery called them in, and his own, and other fighter groups went into action. Despite "kneeing" his gun-sight switch to the Off position, he engaged and destroyed two Bf 109s before realizing that his sight was malfunctioning. Switching it on again he took out an Fw 190 during a head-on pass. Lieutenant Harley Brown (55th Fighter Squadron) equaled this figure, as did Lieutenant Fiebelkorn. The latter added to the 77th Fighter Squadron total by shooting down two out of four Bf l09s landing at their base, as well as chasing a third down to ground-level and finishing it off. Captain Tennant (55th Fighter Squadron) also scored three kills. Bf 109 "deuces" were credited to Lieutenant Mansker (55th Fighter Squadron) and Lieutenants Rowlett, Jones and Schallo (all 77th Fighter Squadron). With eight other pilots scoring individual kills some twenty-eight Luftwaffe fighters had been destroyed.

One pilot was being hard pressed by seven Bf l09s when a 4th Fighter Group P-51 knocked down one and distracted the others. Not so lucky were Captain Serros (55th Fighter Squadron Leader), and the 77th Fighter Squadron's Lieutenant Kennedy and Lieutenant Van Woert. Serros did not survive his bail out over the Zuiderzee, while Kennedy also said he was baling out, but being west of Ostend probably landed, and perished, in the North Sea. He is commemorated on the "Wall of the Missing" at Henri-Chapelle Cemetery, Holland. Van Woert was missing after the air battle and was later reported as KIA.

Merseburg (8 November) witnessed another Me 262 incident when Lieutenant Fiebelkorn gave chase to one; as he positioned to fire, another P-51 intruded. Immediately the jet fighter began to spin and went into the ground. Neither P-51 had fired so the reason for the crash remained a mystery.

Dive-bombing power stations the next day proved costly. First Lieutenant Wilson (77th Fighter Squadron) having released his bomb, had a wing separate as he pulled away and went in. Then Lieutenant Loetscher (55th Fighter Squadron) tight-turned after strafing, flipped over on his back and crashed. On a happier note, Lieutenant Colonel Randolph's (Deputy Group Commander) transfer to command the 359th Fighter Group at East Wretham. The group was an element of the 67th Fighter Wing along with the 20th Fighter Group.

This P-51D Mustang, MC-B of the 79th Fighter Squadron, was named *Snuggle Bunny*. (via Larry Davis)

On 10 November, Colonel Rau nearly "bought the farm" during an armed recce run to Czechoslovakia. His oxygen hose disconnected, the P-51 went into a dive and the engine quit. Many of thousands feet lower, he managed to reconnect the hose and began to function normally as well as regaining power. Another duty recently assigned the 20th Fighter Group was to escort Photo Reconnaissance (PR) aircraft, the first mission taking place on 16 September. The second mission on 20 November involved ten P-51s split in two groups to cover a Spitfire to Koblenz and Frankfurt and two P-38s to Berlin. Captain Ilfrey led this second flight with Lieutenant Keiso as his wingman.. Bad weather forced this flight to return at low-level and all landed in Belgium - all five pilots that is, despite there only being four aircraft. Lieutenant Kelso's P-51 was laying behind enemy lines close to Maastricht!

The small formation had been engaged by flak at Maastricht and Lieutenant Kelso's P-51 was hit and lost power. A convenient clearing housing what seemed to be an emergency strip loomed ahead and Ilfrey called Kelso to use his own judgment in making either a wheels-down or wheels up landing. The Lieutenant chose "wheels-down" and brought his aircraft to a precarious halt right at the strip's end. Although Ilfrey later expressed his determination to attempt a "pick-up" right at the onset of the incident, the fact that a proper landing could apparently be made surely bolstered that determination.

Kelso's P-51 was under ground-fire so he cleared away from it as Ilfrey made his approach. After a successful touch-down, Ilfrey got out on the wing to discard his harness while Kelso got into the Mustang. Ilfrey now sat in Kelso's lap but discovered that with two pair of legs extended on the floor he could not reach the rudder pedals. Kelso repositioned himself in a cross-legged position, but even so Ilfrey could hardly lower himself enough for the canopy to close. With his neck bent and knees drawn up he cracked open the throttle for a very bumpy take-off. The final difficulty occurred as Ilfrey went to pull back the control-column, when he, in his own words, "almost emasculated myself." In the air, the P-51 was headed towards Brussels and a safe landing. His subsequent reception on return to Kingscliffe was somber, since actions, such as he had taken were not encouraged, since it might (and on some occasions did) mean that not one but two pilots were lost. The unoffi-

BUTCH, a P-51D of the 79th Fighter Squadron, had three kill markings painted on the canopy frame , The fuselage national insignia was Grayed out, (Via Larry Davis)

A pair of Mustangs of the 79th FIghter Squdron fly formation with a third aircraft. The Mustang in the foreground (MC-B) was named *"Panty Waste"*. (Via Larry Davis)

cial response, however, was usually more positive.

The next day's mission to Merseburg was being launched when Lieutenant Reichard (79th Fighter Squadron) raced down the runway and pulled back his control column only to have the P-51 loose power. The propeller and one drop-tank impacted with the runway but Reichard managed to hold the damaged fighter in the air while jettisoning the one remaining tank. He took up a heading for Wittering and a safe touchdown. Lieutenant Robb (77th Fighter Squadron) aborted with jammed guns deep in enemy territory and a stuck drop-tank. His wingman Lieutenant Halpin stayed with him but near Osnabruck they were jumped by five Bf 109s and Fw 190s. They broke in opposite directions and although Robb was seriously handicapped he managed to evade his tormentors. In contrast Halpin was jumped by three of the enemy and finally ended up in Stalag Luft III.

Routine escort duties on six occasions closed off the month. Among those finishing their tours were Lieutenant Colonel Low, Captain Scrutchfield (55th Fighter Squadron) and Captain Yaryan (79th Fighter Squadron). Low had arrived in April and assumed Squadron Commander status after a spell as Squadron Operations Officer. Both Captains had joined the Group in late 1942 and all three had an average of 270 hours operational flying.

Confined in a noisy, cramped cockpit for many hours did not permit the pilot much in the way of relaxation. For example, it was always a relief to unhook the tight fitting oxygen mask. In Lieutenant Harley Brown's (55th Fighter Squadron) case he would sometimes light up a cigarette, an action which almost cost him his life when returning off a mission at low level. Having lit up, he then came across a locomotive and instinctively rammed the control column forward to sight his target. With his seat harness straps having also been loosened his body was automatically thrust up against the canopy. Worse still, his dinghy pack twisted sideways and jammed him in his elevated position. He was in serious trouble.

The cigarette now clenched in his mouth, he frantically used both hands to work the pack back into position. As death in the form of the onrushing locomotive loomed up, his frantic efforts succeeded allowing him to pull back on the stick to barely clear his intended target. The locomotive did not survive his second strafing run, but that was the end of the fortunate pilot's cockpit smokes.

Following the disaster at Arnhem in September it became obvious that the War in Europe would drag on into 1945. The Allies could only consolidate their front-line until a Spring Offensive could be launched. Hitler had very different plans and the Battle of the Bulge action in mid-December at one point threatened the very core of Allied military intentions.

This P-51D of the 79th Fighter Squadron has the seial number painted just below the unit marking on the tail. (via Larry Davis)

With Anglo-American forces entrenched in Belgium and Southern Holland the pressure on pilots with mechanical trouble or combat damage eased considerably. Now they would not have to automatically "sweat out" the crossing of the North Sea as was the case prior to D-Day and for the initial first weeks after the invasion when most of France was still occupied. On 2 December Lieutenant Hall (77th Fighter Squadron) suffered engine problems and bellied-in near Brussels. He was seriously burnt in the crash landing. His wingman, Lieutenant Joseph, failed to emerge from the undercast into which they had previously descended and a cemetery plot in the Ardennes was his sad destiny.

During August, the Group had had the highest percentage of assigned aircraft available for combat in the 67th Fighter Wing, as well as the highest number of kills and the best kill/loss ratio. Now in December, it led the entire 8th Fighter Command in the first statistic, while leading the Wing in aircraft serviceability and the least number of aborts. In the kill/loss ratio it was second in the Command. The men behind the men who made the headlines had striven through a dreadful initial spell of mechanical difficulties to reach and sustain this pinnacle of operational success. The Winter of 1944/45 was adjudged one of the worst in England for many years. Flying single-engine fighters was risky enough in clear weather but when snow storms and ice were added to solid undercasts or overcasts that risk was greatly enhanced. Flying in cloud for any length of time could easily induce vertigo, while the turbulent nature of cumulus-nimbus cloud would lead to the destruction of many individual aircraft and on occasions to entire Flights. There was ever the danger of straying off course and heading to the south of the British Isles to finish up (if lucky) over enemy territory or (if unlucky) out into the Atlantic. Even when regaining friendly shores, descending through cloud could lead a pilot into high ground or unforeseen obstructions such as barrage balloons. The average fighter pilot's transparently breezy manner was often a shield for more sober reflections. He was pilot, navigator and gunner rolled into one with nobody but himself to assist if he ran into trouble.

Aerial combat in December would be very sparse with the mission on 2 December the sole occasion when enemy fighters would be challenged or even sighted. A brace of Fw 109s were credited to Lieutenant Harley Brown with Lieutenants Murrel and Garner (77th Fighter Squadron) sharing the second. On the other hand, several Group pilots were lost. On 6 December, Lieutenant Katz (77th Fighter Squadron) crashed near Ipswich while aborting and four days later Lieutenant Urbanski (55th Fighter Squadron) was seen to dive into cloud near Frankfurt. Urbanski had only been assigned on 28 October and had flown just over forty combat hours when he was KIA. In stark contrast Colonel Harold Rau had flown 275 combat hours since assignment on 20 March and had led the 356th Fighter Group before arriving to command the 20th Fighter Group. He was now returning home, having been feted during a farewell party on 9 December.

This was the second P-51D Mustang to carry the name *Gumpy*. Lieutenant Colonel Montomgery was assigned the aircraft in January of 1945 and it survived the war to be scrapped during 1946, The P-51D has four kill markings on the canopy rail.

The Battle of the Bulge began on 16 December with Von Rundstedt's push through the Ardennes and on to Antwerp coinciding with thick weather conditions which grounded the Allied Air Forces and kept them from any direct counter-thrusts against the enemy armored columns. The strategic bombers were still able to strike at German industry, however, although their efforts over the succeeding seven days were restricted to three full missions. The 20th Fighter Group participated in all but two. Captain Pubentz (79th Fighter Squadron) flew his final mission on 18 December. Turning back with engine trouble, all power went while over France. His initial decision to force land after jettisoning his canopy was altered in favor of bailing out, his parachute descent depositing him on the ground uninjured.

The land campaign's ninth day opened with blessedly clear skies and the scene was set for the 8th and 9th Air Forces to launch the greatest number of aircraft bombing to date. The targets were airfields and communication centers behind the battle-lines. The RAF also dispatched over 500 Lancasters and Halifaxes to supplement these assaults. Now with the exception of 28 December, daily missions were sent out and the 20th Fighter Group was in on them all. Over seventy P-51s made the Christmas Eve mission, although fog over the Midlands forced the pilots to divert to Wormingford, home of the 55th Fighter Group. An average of fifty-four fighters were dispatched on the final six December missions, but there were seven aborts. On 31 December, eight of these taking off escorted photo-reconnaissance P-38s over SW Germany.

By the beginning of 1945 the Luftwaffe was all but spent as an effective opposition to the virtually daily incursions into the Reich's heartland by the USAAF bombers and their escorts. An added pressure was the equally regular presence of the RAF's Lancasters and Halifaxes by day as well as by night.

Rail and road communications were featured targets during the first few January days as the task of driving back the German forces in the Ardennes was completed. Given the lengthy nature of many missions for the fighters, this forced even greater reliance on consuming all their fuel, particularly the fuel contained in drop tanks. Should those tanks be prematurely jettisoned, the subsequent flight to the target and home could become too close for comfort. Six pilots experienced this limitation on 1 January when they tackled two Me 262's which made a slashing attack near Madgeburg. Having jettisoned, they barely made the return leg back to the Allied side of the battle-lines. One of these 55th Fighter Squadron pilots was Flight Officer Sheffield, who two days later ran out of luck, turning back with coolant problems and baling out (it is believed) between Belgium and England. An ASR search proved fruitless and his name appears on the "Wall of the Missing" at Henri-Chapelle Cemetery, Holland.

Separate "A" and "B" formations were sent on 6 January with eight other Mustangs serving in a PR escort role, for a total of sixty P-51s. This figure was fairly average for the Group and reflected the unit's continued pre-eminence within the 8th Fighter Command for aircraft available for combat; also, its abort rate was the second lowest in the 8th Fighter Command.

Oil targets on 14 January promised some form of determined, if limited, opposition. Sure enough near Berlin, Major Nichols called in several gaggles of Fw 190s and Bf 109s and Major Gatterdam, leading the "B" Group (55th and 77th Fighter Squadrons) attacked. Almost simultaneously Nichols sighted another large gaggle hitting a preceding bomber formation and he led "A" Group into contact. In what would be one of the final fighter versus fighter contests, the 20th Fighter Group left the Luftwaffe some nineteen and a half aircraft fewer. Major Gatterdam was under grave threat from an Fw 190, when Lieutenant Jake Brown answered his call for help and clobbered the German fighter. Gatterdam

An unidentified member of the 381st Bomb Group sets in the cockpit of a 77th Fighter Squadron P-51B Mustang during the Spring of 1945. The Mustang carries a single kill on the fuselage below the cockpit.

then went on to knock down two other Fw 190s as his contribution, achieving Ace status in the process (the half kill related to one that was shared with a 4th Fighter Group pilot).

A few weeks earlier, Lieutenant Harley Brown had experimented with firing his guns while inverted, an action which threw the P-51 into a series of spins costing 15,000 feet. Having worked out the correct recovery procedure which cost but a fraction of that height, he now was engaging a Bf 109. In the frenetic series of maneuvers which followed both fighters stalled-out. Thanks to his spin practice he was able to maintain his position behind the Bf 109 instead of falling ahead of it. Despite further tight turns, dives and climbs by the German pilot, actions which had Brown dumping full flap and even lowering his landing gear, he finally struck the Bf 109 around the fuel tank, exploding it. This was one of two kills scored this day which also elevated him to Ace status. He later acknowledged that this joust was the toughest to date. The Clan Brown were busy because Lieutenant Jake Brown also shot down two fighters.

The twisted wreck of KI-C of the 55th Fighter Squadron after Lieutenant Walter Schrcbeck crash while landing at Leiston on 1 May 1945. The aircraft flipped and nearly ripped the tail section from the fuselage. (via Larry Davis)

Strafing runs north of Munster on 17 January cost the liberty of Lieutenant Planchak (55th Fighter Squadron); having lost engine coolant from flak strikes, he was last seen with jettisoned canopy and going into a dive. He bailed out and ended up in enemy hands. So far the fighters assigned to PR escort had seen little action. On 21 January, during a run over Stettin, the four 79th Fighter Squadron pilots involved in the photo escort had to ward off passes on the PR Mosquito by performance superior Me 262s, some fourteen of them. The action ended in a draw to great relief all round, but there was little doubt that the P-51 was no match for the Me 262 in direct combat, especially when many were flown by the cream of the Luftwaffe.

February of 1945 opened with continued attacks on transportation and oil resources with Berlin being hard hit on 2 February to hinder Wehrmacht traffic channeling through to the Eastern Front. The fourth full month's mission was an escort to Lutzkendorf which was quiet for all but the 77th Fighter Squadron led by Major Gilbertson. Unlike the other two squadrons who were impeded by the undercast in dropping down for strafing, the 77th Fighter Squadron managed to penetrate near

Esperstadt. Lieutenant Larson started what amounted to a massacre by blowing up one of two Fw 190s; other pilots joined indiscriminately until Gilbertson called for a left-hand pattern of attack and evasion in view of the ever-increasing smoke clouds billowing from numerous burning wrecks. In some twenty minutes, thirty-nine aircraft were smashed or burned, with Captains Einhaus and Cole scoring twelve between them. One of the three Fw 190s credited to Gilbertson blew up in his flight-path, shattering a sizable portion of the canopy and wounding him in the forehead.

That score might have been increased had not most of the squadron been short on ammunition. The retiring squadron ran into fifteen Bf 109s shortly after disengaging at Espenstadt. What claims were entered at Kingscliffe were few and were all in the damaged category. They involved Captain Jennings and Lieutenants Purse, Hall and Schallo. Lieutenant Nuno failed to return, being the latest Group pilot to be KIA.

Saint Valentines Day involved a long haul to Dresden with another pilot added to the MIA list; this was Lieutenant Leon (55th Fighter Squadron) who piled in while strafing a truck. Seven other pilots landed on the Continent and Lieutenant Schwarz (79th Fighter Squadron) escaped unscathed when his P-S1 nosed over at Debach. Three Me 262s ran into the 55th Fighter Squadron, one of which was damaged by Captain Jake Brown. The next day the unpredictable English weather struck as the Group took-off, a sudden fog descending to thwart the efforts of the last nine pilots to lift off. On 19 February, strafing runs in the Magdeburg area added ten more locomotives to the destroyed tally, but the string of February losses was continued when Lieutenant Murrell (77th Fighter Squadron) impacted fatally with a tree. One pilot intercepted a Me 410 but missed. The Me 410 (known as the Hornet to its crews) mounted rear firing stinger guns located on the fuselage sides; and in this case several hits were made on the P-51's right wing.

Rail traffic took the brunt of the punishment handed out the next day, but once again a trio of pilot losses occurred involving the 55th Fighter Squadron. A tank car blew up directly in the path of Lieutenant Stitzer who was seen to pull out of the flames and debris with one main gear leg extended prior to rolling over and plunging into the ground. Captain Ford's fighter was so damaged by flak that he had to force land. Lieutenant McGee attempted to emulate Captain Ilfrey's action on 20 November by landing to pick Ford up. He unluckily bent a propeller blade as his P-51's nose pitched down towards the end of his landing run. There was still a chance of getting clear, as the duo sat themselves into the cockpit. However, the soft nature of the field caused one main wheel to sink in and even full power could not drag the aircraft free.

Abandoning his Mustang, McGee accompanied by Ford, ran off into nearby woods but were soon apprehended and imprisoned at Nuremberg. Colonel Rau's admonition to Captain Ilfrey about the risks involved in such an action held added weight, considering what happened on this occasion. Lieutenant McNeel somewhat evened matters up when he shot down a Bf 109. The 77th Fighter Squadron having fired a large train of oil-tankers among other things, added aerial victims to its list when Yellow Flight ran into six light trainers of which four were dispatched. A further three aircraft were torched at Straubling airfield.

But the strafing prize today went to the 79th Fighter Squadron. Weiden airfield was packed with Me 110s and He 111s and the fifteen minute bash by the squadron demolished sixteen of these, along with nineteen being claimed as damaged. Captain Kies was flying what would be his fifty-ninth and final mission. Having destroyed two He 111s on his first pass, he went in again, but was struck by a bullet which entered his right knee and exited through the thigh. His immediate thought was to land on the airfield but he rejected the idea, reasoning that he might either be shot down or not receive proper medical attention from the understandably irate Germans. He turned his rudder trim-tab to a position where the need to use his right leg on the rudder-pedal was rendered unnecessary.

Now came the task of applying a tourniquet; having finally slipped it into position he remembered previous advice to loosen it every fifteen minutes to allow the blood to circulate. His situation was extremely perilous, being deep in Germany and alone. The appearance of two bogeys left him with no choice but to head for a far-off cloud-bank since he could not take any real evasive action in the event they attacked; thankfully he reached the cloud after a few minutes flying with the throttle wide open.

***Miss Miami* was P-51D of the 77th Fighter Squadron that was assigned to Lieutenant Rep Jones. He completed his combat tour in April of 1945, claiming seven kills (both air and ground). The aircraft was scrapped in September of 1945.**

Recurring bouts of semi-consciousness assailed him as he climbed through the cloud, with the added concern that if he were to slip into a spin he could not use his right leg to correct the P-5l's errant course. Not having a clear idea of the course home he called up the Ground Control facility located on the Continent but to no avail. In fact he would first sight the ground as he swung in over the Wash region northeast of Kingscliffe. Calling ahead for medical assistance to be on hand, he was advised to divert into Wittering with its much more generous runway length.

His main landing problem was to prevent the P-51 from swinging too much to the left as its rudder lost effect once the fighter was slowing; also he could not apply even brake pressure with only one leg. Fortunately the P-51's tail-wheel would not swivel provided the control column was held fully back which in turn would assist him to keep a dead-ahead path.

His first approach was thwarted by the simultaneous landing of an RAF aircraft and, although feeling he had not the strength to go round, he was able to complete a landing circuit. A sound touch-down was made to the runway's right-side. Even with full back-pressure applied to the control column to hold the tail-wheel down on the ground Kies' P-51 began to steadily slide to the left and ended up at some 45 degrees to the runway. Unlike the fighter, which was back in service within a few days, its pilot's combat career was over. He spent much of the next two years in the hospital.

Armorers check out the guns on IDIOT'S DELIGHT, of the 77th Fighter Squadron. The crew are (L-R): T/SGT McNivin, S/SGT Lawrence and Corporals Kallas and Kost.

MC-Q of the 79th Fighter Squadron carried the name *POLLY* on the nose in Red, just under the unit marking. (via Larry Davis)

On 22 February, Lieutenants Van Sickle and North (77th Fighter Squadron) came back to Kingscliffe from the Continent having landed there off the 20 February mission. They reported the destruction of three Bf 108 trainers. The third led them back to its airfield where it was downed by Lieutenant Van Sickle (his second) and five of its eight companions on the ground were set on fire. Lieutenant Leonard Wright's combat career began - and ended over Hamburg on 24 February. He suffered engine coolant loss and had to bail out, at least his imprisonment was fated to last but a matter of weeks. His loss was the first the 79th Fighter Squadron had suffered since October of 1944.

Another strafing bonanza occurred on 25 February when seventeen locomotives were taken out along with a number of vehicles. Captain Cole's 55th Fighter Squadron flight caught five Fw 190s taking-off and the Captain clobbered four in quick succession. Swift revenge was exacted on Cole by another Fw 190 which screamed down and damaged his coolant system. A short time later he made a force landing, and was captured.

The 77th Fighter Squadron pilot's assailant was in turn shot down by Major Cristadoro. Further punishment was handed out by Lieutenant Nicholson (an Fw 190) while Captain Freuchtenicht's 55th Fighter Squadron flight bounced thirty Bf 109s flying in between the cloud-layers to score four kills, including two by Lieutenant Kier. Sadly, while returning at ground level, Kier's wingman, Lieutenant H. B. Smith was set on fire by flak and he crashed, with fatal results. A second loss was Captain Cole's No. 4, Lieutenant Soleau, who now lies buried in the Ardennes. The next day was no better with Lieutenant Whitely turning for home with fuel deficiency. He was seen by Lieutenant Kahn, acting as cover, to force land while still over enemy territory. More fortunate was Major Nichols. One of his gun-bays received a direct flak hit on 28 February, which set off some of the ammunition but did no structural damage.

Victory in Sight

By March of 1945, the Allies were poised to strike across Germany's natural Western barrier, the River Rhine. The month opened on a disappointing note for the Group when the bomber formation under the 77th Fighter Squadron's guard was attacked just after bombing, with one B-17 being shot down. Although the squadron promptly engaged the six Fw 190s and two Bf 109s involved only two damaged claims could be submitted by Lieutenants Rep Jones and McAllister, low cloud assisting the enemy fighters to disengage successfully.

Flying their last missions on 4 March, were Captains Howard and Harley Brown (55th Fighter Squadron). The latter pilot had had his narrow escapes during his time at Kingscliffe, one of which proved the point that simple lapses could cost a pilot his liberty or his life. Aborting off a Hamburg mission with a jammed oxygen regulator, Brown jettisoned his almost full drop-tanks as bombs over the city and steadily eased his P-51's path down to around 15,000 feet. Leveling out and applying power he got no response - his engine was dead. Repeated cockpit checks appeared to show nothing amiss. Knowing he could never get home, and being then over the Zuiderzee, he decided to turn back and bailout. One final instrument check fortunately provided the reason for the engine failure, he had not switched over from drop tanks to main tanks. Once the omission was corrected, the Merlin began purring again and the mightily relieved pilot headed westwards to salvation.

In contrast, Major Jack Price was on his first mission with the Group, having done a tour with the 78th Fighter Group at Duxford followed by six months with the 67th Fighter Wing. Another second tour veteran also started the mission on 8 March; this was Captain Bob Riemensnider, now the 55th Fighter Squadron Operations Officer. The mission was No. 276 (No 138 had been the point of conversion to the P-51). Statistics revealed that the kill/loss ratio of the P-51 was five times that of the P-38. On the other hand the chances of aerial combat for the latter were arguably never as clear-cut while the strafing role (and therefore the opportunity to score ground kills) was regularly assigned well into the period of P-38 operations. Nevertheless, the change-over appeared to have been generally welcomed.

Yet another exotic German design was encountered on 15 March. This was the Me 163 rocket-fighter, two being met by two flights headed by Colonel Gustke. The Mustang's could not match the fantastic rate of climb of the Me 163s. Flight Officer Shaffer had earlier aborted with engine trouble and was subsequently heard to say that all power had gone; he did not survive.

Me 262s were encountered on 20 and 21 March missions. On 20 March, twelve to fifteen of the jet fighters challenged the bomber-stream. None were downed but two were damaged by Lieutenants Nicholson (55th Fighter Squadron) and John Cowley (77th Fighter Squadron). A group of eight jets were wrongly identified as friendly by Captain Michel (55th Fighter Squadron) on 21 March; fortunately he realized his error as he neared his "friends." Lieutenant Swiercynski (77th Fighter Squadron) landed on the Continent; three days later he was captured, becoming a POW.

The day of Swiercynski's loss was a momentous occasion, signaling the launch of operation VARSITY, the crossing of the Rhine. Massive parachute drops were made ahead of the Anglo-American armies fording the broad waters in the Ruhr region. The Group flew three missions, their brief being to sweep the Munster/Osnabruck/Gutersloh triangle with the intention of preventing any ground reinforcement by the

Major Walter Yarborough was appointed 79th Fighter Squadron Commander. He was preparing to take off on what would be the last mission flown by the group on 25 April 1945.

Germans, as well as combating any aerial forces. No interceptions were made in the air, although the second mission pilots had barely handed over to the 357th Fighter Group when the latter ran into the Luftwaffe and downed sixteen. Ground targets proved almost as scarce.

Colonel Gustke made one pass at Gutersloh airfield to damage a Ju 88; otherwise one truck on the last mission was the only other claim. No matter, because the main purpose of the land operation was achieved within hours when ground troops linked up with their Airborne contemporaries. Group records noted that Swiercynski was flying MURPH, a P-51 which had been noted as missing on previous missions but had always turned up later - a hope which was finally in vain. Unknown to the pilots was the fact that only three more would go down in combat with all surviving. Death, however, was to claim one more pilot on 28 March, Lieutenant Pettit failing in an attempted forced-landing near Ipswich. Two veterans completed their tours on 28 and 31 March, Lieutenant Colonel Bob Meyer (79th Fighter Squadron Commander) and Lieutenant Colonel Russell Gustke. This was Meyer's second tour at Kingscliffe, but Gustke went one better. His first combat spell was in North Africa between May of 1942 and Jan of 1943 with the 14th Fighter Group. Joining the 55th Fighter Squadron in September of 1943, he flew with the squadron until transferred to the 20th Fighter Group in February; this composite tour was completed in June of 1944. These two men had flown 1,129 combat hours between them. Also finishing were the Van Sickle brothers Frank and Dick (both 77th Fighter Squadron).

As the Group entered April, the final run of eighteen missions the Group would fly was to be virtually free of contact with the Luftwaffe. Apart from one jet, which landed hits on Lieutenant Papuzynski's P-51 (77th Fighter Squadron), only the mission on 16 and 17 April involved air-to-air contact, although the occasion would be memorable. Before that stage the final incident calling for ASR intervention occurred on 4 April. Lieutenant Cudd (77th Fighter Squadron) had his engine catch fire following coolant-loss and jumped when thirty miles off Great Yarmouth. He was circled by three P-51s while Lieutenant Huey located an ASR launch nearby and guided it to the spot.

Just after bombs away at Oranienburg on 10 April, between ten and fifteen jet fighters attacked. In the ensuing melee, the Group accounted for five of the jets. Recovering from his recent drenching, Lieutenant Cudd shared one with Flight Officer Rosenblum. Two other 77th Fighter Squadron pilots, Lieutenants Drozd and Hall also scored, while the 55th Fighter Squadron's Lieutenant J. K. Brown and the 79th Fighter Squadron's Captain Hollins also got one each. In return the last three pilots to go "into the bag" were downed over Fossberg airfield. Captain Tracy and Lieutenant Peterburg (55th Fighter Squadron) and Lieutenant Stewart (79th Fighter Squadron) were the unlucky trio. But they had already destroyed four, five and seven aircraft respectively before succumbing to flak; Lieutenant Peterburg was on his sixth run when taken down. Their successes were mirrored by other pilots who added thirty-eight more to the destroyed total, along with twenty-three listed as damaged. Lieutenant Colonel Montgomery bagged three, but Lieutenant Jurgens (79th Fighter Squadron) led the pack with eight destroyed.

The last air combats took place on 17 April. These again involved Me 262s but only two pilots got close enough to shoot. Lieutenant Scott (79th Fighter Squadron) landed strikes on one before the pilot applied power to out distance the P-51. Flight Officer Rosenblum had damaged a second and was closing in when four other P-51s cut across his path and prevented any further contact.

Ground targets were equally scarce. The occasional locomotive was hit as on 13 April and a single aircraft was destroyed on 16 April, Lieutenant King and Major Gilbertson (77th Fighter Squadron) being the pilots concerned. The sole two-man P-51 sortie was flown on 19 April when Captain Mansker carried Captain Hank Howard (Asst Group Intelligence Officer) in the Group's "Piggy-back" P-51B. The mission to Falkenburg was quiet which was maybe just as well for the supernumerary crewman. At least he gained a sight of Berlin after the Group were diverted in that direction in search of reported enemy fighters - a report which turned out to be false. The Skoda plant at Pilsen was the assigned target on 25 April. This mission was Major Gilbertson's 100th, while Lieutenant Gjolme (also 77th Fighter Squadron) was starting his second tour. Take-off was 0725 and the bombers were covered in the target area and back to Frankfurt when the Group withdrew back to

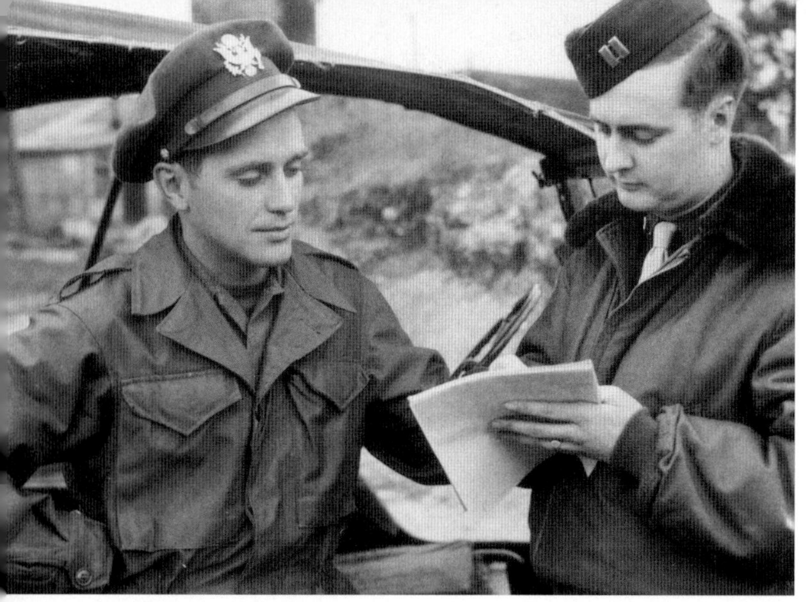

A thinner faced Captain "Slick" Morris of the 77th Fighter Squadron is debriefed by Captain Barkley, an intelligence officer, after his release from Stalag Luft I, at Barth, Germany. He had been captured on 7 July 1944.

England. Lieutenant Bishop (79th Fighter Squadron bailed out near Dusselldorf but landed safely in Allied hands, but only after nearly descending into a tall chimney.

The aerial war for the Anglo-American Bombing Offensive was effectively over although thirteen more days would elapse before the Germans signed the Instruments of Surrender. No more miserable days and nights out in the damp atmosphere of the Midlands for the devoted ground crews; no more sweating out early morning take-offs in what were often minimal weather conditions; no more wearying runs over Central Europe. Above all, no more constant threat to life or liberty for the fortunate survivors. The Nazi lust for power was finally and, at great material and human cost, irrevocably shattered.

The Group had acquitted itself well over seventeen months of combat. A total of 312 missions were flown involving 6,847 P-38 and 9,015 P-51 sorties. Some twenty-eight pilots had achieved Ace status with 211 enemy aircraft shot down and 232 destroyed on the ground. Exactly 400 locomotive kills confirmed the "Loco-busters" title along with a host of freight wagons, trucks and other assorted ground targets. These achievements were made at the human cost of seventy-one pilots killed and fifty-four who ended up in POW Camps. Ten other pilots shot down managed to evade capture and regain Allied lines.

These bald statistics are but a background to a tale of endeavor and courage in the face of a skillful foe, as well as manifold problems with the equipment in which the pilots were initially launched into combat. Their memory, along with the ground personnel who provided unremitting support, is perpetuated by a band of Englishmen whose efforts in conjunction with the 20th Fighter Group Association created a fine Memorial at Kingscliffe during 1983. This will stand as a permanent recognition of the Men of America who came a long way from Home to "Live in Fame or Go down in Flame" in their defense of freedom.

For some seventy-one members of the 20th Fighter Group, this is how the war ended. Lieutenant Ferdinand E. Lefevre was Killed In Action (KIA) over Rochecorbon, France on 28 April 1944. After the war ended, he was given a proper service with full military honors at the American Military Cemetery at Neuville-en-Condroz, Liege, Belgium, on 17 October 1945.

First Lieutenant of the
American Air Forces

Ferdinand E. LEFEVRE

Double Air Medal
Double Distinguished Flying Cross.
born at Détroit - Michigan
United States
THE 11 NOVEMBER 1921
killed in action at Rochecorbon
(Indre et Loire -- France)
THE 28 APRIL 1944
buried at the American Military
Cimetery at Neuville-en-Condroz
(Liège - Belgium)
THE 17 OCTOBER 1945